REGIONAL DEVELOPMENT AND THE INTERNATIONAL DIVISION OF LABOUR

REGIONAL DEVELOPMENT AND THE INTERNATIONAL DIVISION OF LABOUR

International firms in the Netherlands and India

Ger van den Broek,
Detlev Haude,
Fons van der Velden

CONCEPT PUBLISHING COMPANY, NEW DELHI-110059

ISBN 81-7022-283-4

First Published 1989

Published by
Ashok Kumar Mittal
Concept Publishing Company
A/15-16, Commercial Block, Mohan Garden
NEW DELHI-110059 (India)

Lay out by
W. Jansen
Department of Planning and Organization
Catholic University of Nijmegen

Printed by
D.B. Offset Works
B-218, Naraina Ind. Area
NEW DELHI-110028

Preface

On the face of it it seems easy to explain how this book has come about. Three people sharing common interests and work experiences get together to co-publish a book on part of their work. This has been the case indeed, however, the backgrounds of this cooperation outreach what is suggested at first sight.

Since its foundation in 1973, the Third World Centre (DWC) has striven for making the scholarly work done at universities accessible to society at large. Over the years this goal has more and more faded into the background of the activities of the Third World Centre indeed, - a development we are merely stating here, we do not rate it - yet the original idea that academic activities should not take place in a social vacuum was still alive. Parallel with developments at universities, Centres for Development Education (COS) emerged as an expression of a growing interest in developing countries; this also happened in Nijmegen. The aim of these centres is to offer material and know-how concerning development issues to labour unions and action groups. When the Centre for Development Education in Nijmegen started a project on the role of international firms in the Nijmegen region, it became possible to enter into a cooperation with the staff and students of the Third World Centre. Under the supervision of the staff of both the DWC and the COS students deepened their knowledge of the history of some multinational corporations in the Nijmegen region. Part of their findings were incorporated in chapter 3 in this publication.

The realization of this cooperation made all the people who were involved feel that they had done their bit towards a communication between academic knowledge and society-oriented education, especially with regard to the labour unions.

We hope the publication of this book will not mark the end but the beginning of a cooperation in those fields where learning and society-oriented education can help each other to raise a political consciousness.

In this case the cooperation has resulted in putting (too) rigid patterns of thought concerning issues on developed versus under-developed, or First versus Third World, into their proper perspective. At the same time the differences between the former colonies and the mother countries have been brought into focus by looking at a phenomenon which will have a growing impact on either future : the international firm.

This book tries to give a modest contribution to the debate on industrialisation, developent and employment falling under the heading of internationalization of economies across borders.

Introduction

The last few decades have witnessed the emergence of a new international division of labour, a change in the geographical pattern of specialization on a global scale. This edition which is a translation of several chapters of a book published in Dutch in 1987, describes this process in general and its impact on one area (Nijmegen, the Netherlands) and on one Third World country (India) in particular.

The book was the outcome of research done by students and staff of the Third World Centre (Catholic University of Nijmegen) and the staff of the Centre for Development Education (COS), who have been analysing the impact of multinationals in the developing world. The COS does action research into the economic structure of the Nijmegen region and uses its results for educational and informational activities within the labour unions and regional action groups. To combine specialist knowledge and to overcome their individual limitations, the two centres set up a joint research project in 1984. The project concentrated on the influence of multinationals on the economic structure of the Nijmegen region and on its working population.

The Nijmegen region is of particular interest since it has one of the highest unemployment rates in the Netherlands and at the same time its economic structure is affected to a great extent by subsidiaries of multinationals. This has to do with the relatively late and uneven industrialisation of this region within the Dutch context. As far as job creation is concerned, regional dependence on multinationals is evident in several cases, which also reflect the growing competition amongst regions within the European Community as well as on a global scale. Certainly, this competition is a reason why the city's council tries to attract multinational corporations by offering investment incentives in the form of good infrastructure, tax exemptions and financial support, which are partly subsidized by the central Government of the Netherlands. Whether or not such policies will result in a broad industrial base for the Nijmegen region _ aimed at electronic high-tech _ remains to be seen.

An analysis of the economic history and structure of the Nijmegen region triggers some tempting comparisons with similar developments in (regions in) developing countries. Obviously, it would be too easy to put Nijmegen and a Third World region on the same level, however, what they do have in common is their dependence on international investments and the competition which may arise between them in this process as well as their uneven economic structure.

For the labour unions, be it in the Netherlands and Nijmegen, or in a developing country, the aforementioned developments and structures pose particular problems. Very often, multinational corporations seem to be the only firms able and willing to invest at all in under-industrialised regions, however, usually they do not fuel a massive increase in jobs. Moreover, the danger of transfer of production facilities when necessitated by corporate strategies is always lurking in the background.

We hope this publication will give academics, trade unionists and other people interested in the subject who haven't read the Dutch publication an introduction to the problems of a region in the European Community that is not very well known. At the same time we look forward to people contacting us, either with similar or different work experience, which might deepen our knowledge of the material presented in this publication and which might, eventually, result in joint research and publication.

Contents

Chapter 1

GLOBAL SHIFT; RECENT TRENDS IN THE INTERNATIONAL DIVISION OF LABOUR

Fons van der Velden

THE "OLD" INTERNATIONAL DIVISION OF LABOUR

The term "division of labour", as originally defined by the eighteenth century economist Adam Smith, refers to the specialization of labourers in different stages of a production process. Hence, initially this concept did not have a geographical meaning. However, earlier on a *geographical* specialization had taken place, which got more emphasis during the colonial period. From then on "*the international division of labour*" was the common expression. Within this division the colonies were the suppliers of *raw materials* and *agricultural* produce, which were shipped to Europe and the USA, and later to Japan as well, where they were converted into industrial commodities. Subsequently, these products were sold in the developed countries as well as the colonies. The first stage of this process was mainly concerned with the control of *raw materials* (mines and plantations), later with the control of *outlets*. Machine-made goods from the West were launched in many colonies, where they often ruined the existing trades and limited industrial activities.

The destruction of *Indian textile industry* by British cotton goods is the best-known example of this process. As a result, in the nineteenth century India's function as a supplier of goods changed to being that of a market. Till the beginning of the nineteenth century the flow of goods from Great Britain to India was rather insignificant. In later years it increased rapidly. For example, in 1815 the export of cotton goods from Great Britain to India went up from about one million yards to 45 million in 1830 and to 100 million in 1939. During this period there was substantial trade in one direction. British goods could be imported duty-free into India, but for Indian goods Britain had erected a tariff barrier. Moreover, direct trade between India and other (European) countries was obstructed. Therefore, this increasing trade from Great Britain to India was not only based on the superiority of machine production, but it was mainly due to direct government interference by Britain in the form of discriminatory tariffs with respect to Indian goods. The export of British cotton goods increased enormously, and by 1850 India, which had exported these same goods for centuries, imported one quarter of British cotton produce. A similar process took place with respect to silk items, iron, pottery, glass and paper.

An important consequence of this massive import from Great Britain was the *de-industrialisation* of India. The urban crafts and the village industries declined and were not compensated by the development of modern industry. Because of the destruction of the Indian export market and the domination of the domestic trade by the British, the Indian population became more and more dependent on agriculture. It had dramatic effects: large cities such as Dacca (now capital of Bangladesh), were almost completely depopulated, on the countryside the traditional balance between indigenous industries and agriculture was upset and the country was increasingly struck by severe famine. Hence, it was during this period that in India a shift from industry to agriculture took place and as a result an enormous pressure was placed on agriculture. During this period, labour did not have an equal value in colonizing and colonized countries. In the latter labour costs were suppressed by force (i.e. on plantations), slavery or other forms of control. That's why the phenomenon of the free wage-labourer as seen in the West, could not exist in India. What this all meant was that the colonies supplied their raw materials at low prices, whereas they were forced to buy industrial products from the West at high prices. As a result of the low wages, the buying power of labourers was suppressed in the colonies.

As is outlined above, this traditional division of labour contributed to the fact that the colonizing powers (i.e. Great Britain from the end of the seventeenth century and Holland during the second half of the nineteenth century) could experience an accelerated industrialisation, whereas most colonies were left with devastated, plundered and stagnant economies, from which they still suffer the consequences.

THE NEW INTERNATIONAL DIVISION OF LABOUR

After World War II and during the mid-1960s in particular, important changes occurred in the above described relations between the industrialised countries and the former colonies, euphemistically mostly called developing countries.

Especially the *labour-intensive industries*, such as leather-working, textiles, clothing and electronics, were transferred from Western Europe to the developing countries. The outcome of these developments is called the *new international division of labour*. This dynamic process of shifting plants from one country or region to another was a logical result of technological changes and economic processes in Western Europe as well as the Third World.

As we will see in chapter 2, a number of developments *in the Netherlands* added significantly to the realization of this process (the so-called *push factors*). Among them are the labour shortage and the fact that after a period of a tightly controlled wage policy, a considerable rise in industrial pay was noted in the Netherlands. These developments contributed to the internationalization of national enterprises. Still now, the large supply of labour and the ever low wage costs and, to a lesser extent, the low price of raw materials are the *pull factors from the Third World.* As is shown in the diagram below, the sharp contrast in wage costs between the developed countries and the Third World still exists.[1]

Hourly Earnings in Manufacturing (US dollars, 1978)

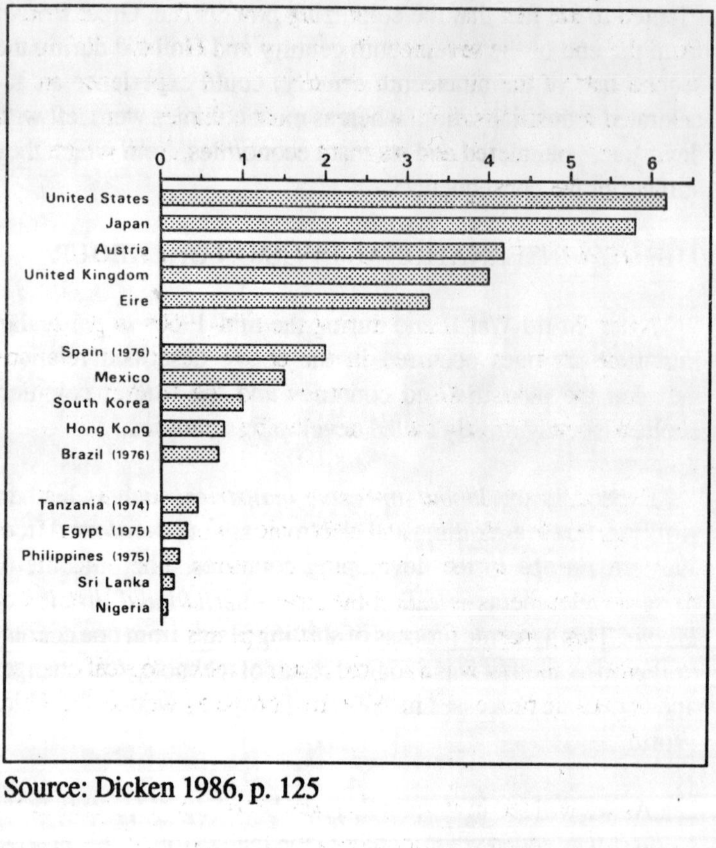

Source: Dicken 1986, p. 125

The industrial policies of the Third World countries themselves were also a major influence in attracting foreign investors. Broadly speaking, two strategies in the industrial policies of the developing countries can be distinguished: import substitution and export-led growth. For each country at a different time, either one or the other may have the upper hand. When after World War

II they had gained political independence, most developing countries opted for a policy of *import substitution.* The emphasis was on the home manufacture of previously imported goods, thus creating their own industrial base in order to become less dependent on Western countries. During this period it was difficult for foreign investors to start their activities in the countries which had just become independent. Besides, the policy of import substitution led to a tight control of foreign currencies, by which the transfer of profits from a subsidiary to the parent company was hampered, if not made impossible. Furthermore, many foreign companies feared nationalization by the host country. In many Third World countries, however, the import substitution policy was a failure. Some of the major causes of that failure were, amongst others, the absence of a sufficiently large domestic market, the emergence of a technological gulf dividing the developed and the developing countries and the problems concerning the balance of payments.

Accordingly, by 1965, *export-led industrialisation* became the new development strategy of developing countries in Latin America and Asia. This strategy was strongly advocated by international Western-dominated organizations such as World Bank and the United Nations Industrial Development Organization (UNIDO). In this new model of development the assumption is that an increase in exports will encourage economic growth. Then, the investments of foreign enterprises have to provide foreign capital and technical know-how. To guarantee a free flow of capital and goods across the borders, protective tariff barriers should be removed. Foreign investors must be given the assurance that they can export their profits from the country and favourable conditions (such as exemption from taxation etc.) are offered to them.

In many Third World countries *Free Trade Zones* were set up. These are areas zoned off by the Government, usually close to an airport or a harbour, where production is for export use only. In these enclaves companies are (to a great extent) exempt from taxation on imports and exports, and other tax advantages and special regulations hold good, such as a ban on labour union actions. In 1966 Free Trade Zones existed in only four Third World countries (Hong Kong, South Korea, Taiwan and Mexico). In 1975 as many as 24 countries had such areas and, by now, there is a worldwide spread of more than 100 Free Trade Zones, where well over one million people are employed. Although percentages differ for each country, a proportion of over 70 percent of the labour force consists of women (most of them young).

The occurence of these interconnected *push and pull factors*- as mentioned above resulted in the spread of the new international division of labour. Within this division the *Third World countries* deal with the *labour-intensive* branches of industry whereas the companies with a more *advanced production technology* (and research institutions) can be found *in the West.* Spectacular improvements in *international transport and communication facilities* made it possible to transfer labour-intensive production processes to the low-wage countries and as a result the choice of a location was no longer greatly influenced by the presence of nearby markets. Also, what was important was that developments in the field of production technology allowed for the fragmentation of the complex production process into simple surveyable parts. Therefore, it is correct to speak of "*Global Factory*" and "*Made in Heaven*", for the actual origin of a product is often difficult to ascertain.

In addition to the above factors, other developments at *branch or company level* came into play as well. For example, the selling of some products stagnated in the developed countries. This concerns the production cycle. When a product has sufficiently matured, reduction in production costs (amongst others, wages and raw materials) and marketing considerations (policies of the host country, new outlets) become more important. For that reason markets in the Third World, too, are adding in significance. Hence, attempts were made to conquer new markets in the Third World. This particularly holds for countries with large domestic markets such as Brazil, Mexico, Kenya and India. Local production for local consumption allows companies to serve the local markets more adequately. Furthermore, it should be noted that none of the large companies operating internationally can afford to neglect the competitors' policies. For example, Philips' activities in Taiwan illustrate this; according to Frits Philips, the former Philips president, they started operating there at first because "*the American and Japanese activities had raised the suspicion that there were opportunities for Philips there as well*".

In all, this sums up the major factors which played a role in big shift of industrial production from Western Europe to countries in the Third World in the mid-1960s. Yet, the impact of the various previously mentioned factors on each company, branch of industry, parent and "host country" is different.

GROWING UNEMPLOYMENT AND POLARIZATION ON THE LABOUR MARKET

From the mid-1960s onwards the question "where can what be produced at the highest profit" has got a global dimension. It especially involves companies with a labour-intensive production process operating in the leather and footwear, textile, clothing and electronics branches. Thus, almost all Dutch textile industry disappeared and was shifted to North Africa (Tunisia) and later to the Far East (South Korea, Hong Kong and Taiwan).

The developments outlined in the previous section also had considerable effects on backward regions in Western Europe. Various labour-intensive industries had fostered mainly because of the initially relatively low wages. In the mid-1960s the rise in pay in the Netherlands and surrounding countries caused many entrepreneurs to move their businesses to the Third World, meanwhile, the ones staying behind were exposed to severe foreign competition. Since 1965, in some areas, the rate of employment in the textile and leather industry has dropped by approximately 90 percent, jobs in other sectors such as the clothing and metal industry have been cut by more than half. While during the 1965-1980 period the number of jobs in manufacturing in the Netherlands soared by 17 percent, in some areas a fall by 40 percent was reported (see chapter 2).

It is not easy to show how employment in Western Europe was affected. Some basic trends can be distinguished. A combination of factors such as technological development (automation and mechanization), the international economic crisis and the relocation of jobs in Third World countries, too, has caused the loss of a large number of jobs over the last two decades. Although the negative effects of the transfer of jobs to the Third World on, for instance, employment in the Netherlands should certainly not be overestimated in number, in some specific regions it had a dramatic impact.

A number of areas were left with a high rate of unemployment. At first it was low-skilled labourers, who suffered from the loss of employment. Additionally, besides the polarization of regions, polarization also occurred on the labour market. A small group of highly qualified workers was opposed to a large group of unskilled labourers. And, it goes without saying that in the Netherlands and other Western countries the bargaining power of the labour unions was affected as a consequence of the decline in economic growth, the increasing unemployment, the polarization of the regions and on the labour market.

MULTINATIONAL CORPORATIONS AND NETWORKS

Multinational corporations largely support the process of international restructuring of capital. In the rest of this chapter attention will be paid to how these enterprises operate.

The United Nations simply define multinationals or transnational corporations as follows: "*Enterprises which own or control production or service outside the country in which they are based. Such enterprises are not always private, they can also be cooperatives or state-owned entities*". The relevance of a multinational corporation is primarily the fact that it may control economic activities in more than one country and take advantage of the differences in production possibilities. Although substantial differences exist in the multinationals' impact on and control of each industry, country and region, there are hardly any parts in the world where they do not assert their influence directly or indirectly.

Dicken points out that the standard definition of a multinational as quoted above is formulated too loosely. According to him, only 4 or 5 percent of the multinational corporations can be considered true *international firms*. For instance, 20 percent of all companies operating internationally have subsidiaries in more than 6 countries, 10 percent in more than 11 countries, 5 percent in more than 16 countries and solely 3.4 percent in more than 20 countries. Furthermore, of only a very limited number of companies more than 20 percent of the assets or jobs are abroad. Judged by Dicken's general criteria, companies such as *Ford Motor Company, IBM, ITT, Union Carbide, General Foods, Coca Cola* (all from the United States), *Volkswagen, Siemens, BASF and Hoechst* (from West Germany) and the Dutch companies *Philips, Unilever, Shell and AKZO* are members of the group of "true" multinational corporations.

As a result of the concentration processes in all industrialised countries, multinational corporations have grown more important in recent years. As a matter of fact in the United States as well as in Great Britain approximately 100 companies account for more than one third of the manufacturing output. Despite the fact that large enterprises dominate the economies of the industrialised countries, this has not resulted in the elimination of smaller companies, which even form the key elements of the economy in the developing countries. Today the interrelations between large and small companies are increasingly transcending national boundaries resulting in *international networks* in which international firms, (small) multinationals and national concerns are interlinked. Within such a network various companies are interconnected in a complex way and frequently agreements are made concerning, for example, outlets. The relations within such networks are often realized by international *subcontracting* (see further). Though relatively few empirical data are available on how these networks operate, it is clear anyhow that they strongly distinguish themselves from the forward and backward linkages of "traditional" multinational corporations, in a *qualitative* as well as a *quantitative* sense.

DOMINANCE OF THE INTERNATIONAL ECONOMY

Since World War II, the growth of multinational corporations has been one of the most significant trends. Today these companies figure so largely in the Western world system that they control a substantial part of world trade and restrict the operations of supranational bodies and nation states to a considerable extent. The annual turnover of world's largest companies such as *General Motors, Exxon, Ford Motor Company, IBM, Mobil, General Electric* exceeds the Gross National Products of many Third World countries.

In "*Transnational Corporations in World Development*", a report published in 1983 by the *United Nations Centre on Transnational Corporations* (UNCTC), detailed empirical data are given to account for these general developments. The greater part of direct private investments by multinational corporations takes place in the Western developed countries; about 20-25 percent has been invested in Third World countries. As far as the developing countries are concerned, foreign investments in Brazil, Argentina, Hong Kong, Malaysia, Mexico and Singapore are still growing. Within the economies of some developing countries foreign companies are often playing a crucial or dominant role as employers or producers of manufactured goods (see table).

Share of foreign companies in jobs in manufacture, and manufacturing production of some Third World countries (percentages)

Country	*Jobs*	*Manufacturing Production*
Argentina	10-12	31
Brazil	30	44
Colombia	28	43
India	13	13
Kenya	30-35	—
Malaysia	33	44
Mexico	21	39
Singapore	58	83

Source: UNCTC, 1983, p. 136.

Multinational corporations are also responsible for a large proportion of exports of these countries. For example, the share of multinational corporations in Argentina's exports is larger than 30 percent, in Brazil's 43, in Colombia's larger than 30 percent, in Mexico's 34 percent and in Singapore's 92 percent.

Furthermore, it is a matter of great concern that approximately 40 percent of the world trade today consists of transactions between parent companies and subsidiaries of multinational corporations. For instance, in 1977 more than 45 percent of the imports into the United States was taking place this way. It is the so-called *intrafirm trade* which enables companies to have profits turn up where they are most advantageous to them (for some examples see chapter 3).

Fifteen big multinational corporations (including *Cargill, Unilever, Continental Grain, Nestlé* and *Reynolds*) control 85 to 90 percent of the international markets for raw materials and minerals such as wheat, coffee, corn, pineapple, cotton, tabacco, jute, oil, iron ore and copper. It is no overstatement to say that firms operating internationally do not only control international investments, but also international production, trade, financing and development of technology.

CENTRAL CHARACTERISTICS OF MULTINATIONALS

Although individual multinational corporations may operate in different sectors and may vary in their make-up, on the whole, some of their characteristic features can be distinguished.

Production Range: Multinationals are reigning supreme in those industrial sectors in which marketing and/or advanced production technology play a central part. Very often they are holding monopoly positions in these markets. Through the years many multinational corporations have adopted a policy of product diversification (to put as many as possible different products on the market in order to spread the risk). For example, *Mitsubishi* and *Volkswagen* have set up ranches in Brazil where they produce meat; *ITT, Shell*, and *Ciba-Geigy*, a pharmaceutic company, are operating in the seeds industry. *Hendrix International*, one of the leading Dutch agrobusiness companies, was taken over by *British Petroleum* (BP), one of the largest oil companies in the world. This is one of the reasons why BP came to hold a strong position in the Western European feed market and became one of the prominent producers of day-old chickens. As far as we can see now, some recent changes have taken place in the diversification policy of various companies. The concentration of capital is still going on, however, nowadays it happens through the expansion of the existing product groups.

Outlets: In Third World countries the selling and manufacture of multinational corporations is especially oriented towards new products which agree with the taste and preferences of the high-income brackets. For example, Dutch companies in India are manufacturing clock radios, hifi equipment, cosmetics and tapes. Expansion of outlets is often reached by taking over or merging with existing companies, in contrast to setting up companies of their own.

Production Process: Multinational corporations usually produce their goods in a capital-intensive way, supported by Research & Development within the company itself. Generally, multinationals spend more money on Research & Development than other firms. Research & Development activities are strongly concentrated in the developed countries, for the most part in the country of the company's origin.

Interests of the entire company vs. those of the subsidiaries: What is at stake within a multinational corporation is not the interests of the individual plant but those of the whole company. What should be produced and where it can be produced at the lowest production costs are examined continuously. Then it may happen that the employees of individual plants, regions and countries are played off against one another.

Global spread: Multinational corporations are particularly to be found in big economies with stable political climates. This is due to the so-called capital and labour conditions and to the outlets. In a stable political climate such as Hong Kong, Singapore and Taiwan the Government provides for an adequate industrial infrastructure and a well-disciplined work force. Despite huge differences in income within each country, India, Brazil, Kenya and Mexico are still interesting as outlets because of their size.

Internal organization: Within a multinational company, decision-making with respect to investing, marketing, and research is usually strongly centralized. It is a familiar fact that in large firms in general and in multinational corporations in particular, the internal decision-making structure is strongly hierarchical. The conduct of the individual company can only be understood if it is clear which position it occupies in the whole corporation. It goes without saying that within the imposed structure, most companies do enjoy a certain degree of independence.

Location: The corporate headquarters, the regional headquarters and Research & Development departments of multinational corporations are usually in the developed countries. It is the production units in which the spread is largest. Decisions concerning the location of plants are determined by factors such as the presence and the price of labour and raw materials etc., and the size and the vicinity of outlets. Also, the labour intensity of the product, the degree of standardization and fragmentation of the production process and the government policies in the developed and the developing countries have an impact on the final decision where to locate a plant.

Political influence: Multinational corporations do not operate in a social vacuum, but they are part of political-economic networks in autonomous countries. Consequently, their political influence in developing countries is often significant. They are directly or indirectly affecting the individual policies of many Third World countries.

FORM OF FOREIGN INVESTMENTS

At the time of the colonial rule foreign investments in various colonies were made in the form of portfolio or direct investments. *Portfolio investments*, controlled by the London capital market, consist of investment in shares and bonds of local companies in the colonies by foreigners. Contrary to *direct investments*, this type of investment implied that the investor involved stayed out of the day-to-day affairs of the company.

After World War II, and since the mid-1960s in particular, increased instability in large parts of the Third World had the effect that the control of plants based abroad was exerted in ways other than capital participation. Up until the 1980s three strands of the worldwide expansion can be distinguished. They prove that the "old-fashioned" flow of capital came to play a minor part.

Firstly, companies operating internationally began exploring variety of funds. The traditional method of capital export became less important. Retained profits or depreciation and loans on the local and international capital market became the sources for investment.

Secondly, it is striking that no longer it is big concerns only which are participating in the internationalization of the production, but also middle- and small-size companies from the service sector (banks, engineering firms, insurance companies etc.). The number of countries from where multinational companies operate is growing. It is remarkable that some Third World countries are among them too, such as India, South Korea and Brazil.

Thirdly, a diversification in the form of economic control has taken place. From this time onwards big companies have expanded less and less on a global scale by means of equity share participation, instead however, they have done so more and more by the so-called "*non-equity*" control: transfer of technology, management and marketing agreements etc.

RECENT DEVELOPMENTS: INCREASE IN HOME-WORKING AND SUBCONTRACTING

Affected by recent *technological developments* and *economic crisis*, the form of foreign investments in the Third World and the planning of the production have undergone significant changes again over the last few years. There has also been a considerable growth of the supply of labour in Western Europe. Moreover, a changing demand for labour has emerged. Today entrepreneurs want the production to be planned in such a way that they can promptly react to changes in the market, and supply at short notice.

These developments lead to *restructuring* within some industrial sectors, often by means of international subcontracting (putting out production to other businesses). In the West the number of permanent jobs in industry is declining; flexibility of the labour factor has become a key concept. The part temporary agencies are playing is growing in significance; and an increase in *temporary employment contracts* and *home-working* can be seen.

Affected by a large supply in the labour market, the Netherlands has recently experienced such a considerable rise in *temporary, on-call and nil contracts* (stating that the employee has to be available yet he has no right to a job) that, according to the Ministry for Social Affairs and Employment, a proportion of 30 percent of the total Dutch work force worked on a temporary assignment early 1987. This holds true for women in particular.

For some years now, international firms have considered *subcontracting* as a good alternative for direct investments in the low-wage countries. By 1981, with increasing activities in the Third World, subcontracting had virtually become as important as direct investments. For large-scale companies, there are some clear advantages tied up with subcontracting: it leads to reduction in costs, for in a small-scale company production costs are lower; risks can be shifted on to the small-scale industries; it enables large enterprises to react more adequately to changes in the market and to restrict the power of the organized labour movement (for further details concerning these issues see chapter 3). In small-scale industries in the Third World, labour relations still tend to be feudal and terms of employment are usually pathetic. The pay is too little to live on and too much to die.

For instance, employees of small firms producing *Sunlight* soap for Unilever in India, chiefly women and children, are earning about 10 to 15 Rs per day. According to its management, *Fortune Garment Factory*, a clothing business in Bangkok, is paying its labourers, all women, 50 Bath per day (this is about

Rs 15). This is 15 Bath below the legal minimum wage in Thailand. Who places orders with these kinds of companies? One of the principal customers of *Fortune Garment Factory* is the English *Great Universal Stores* (GUS). Their Dutch subsidiary is Wehkamp. GUS' agent in Bangkok and in other places in the Far East is *Dodwell International*, member of the large British *Inchcape Group*. One of *Fortune Garments*' Dutch customers is *Kan & Co.* from Amsterdam. The firm of *Zeeman, Daarnhouwer*, an Amsterdam trading house and *Wehkamp* again are procuring their textiles from another so-called *sweatshop* in Bangkok, euphemistically named *Phaisarn factory*. The girls working at this factory, usually barely 12 or 13, are earning approximately 30 Bath per day (approx. Rs 10), they are not getting any overtime pay and they are often working night and day to get the orders ready in time.

Another notable trend today is that subcontracting is not only on the increase in the Third World, but also in *Western Europe* and the *United States*. It is becoming common practice that not only clothing, food, furniture, shoes, but also commodities which are not as obvious such as cars and modern electronics are being manufactured at small-scale companies. In *Japan* this has been tradition for ages. The country largely owes its industrial success to these small-scale enterprises. Lucas expresses it aptly: "*Located in backstreets, the components for Nissan car engineering are being made in small family companies, and Honda sheet metal work is being pressed in the front room*". In Europe, especially *England* and *Italy* are first at changing the organization and the location of manufacture. In this context the example of the *Benetton* company is thought to be representative by several researchers. Lucas reports:

"This Italian company which, since the late 1970s, has experienced an enormous growth, supplies commodities to a large number of shops in the United States, Japan and Europe. By using the latest techniques, the head office in Italy immediately know about changes in the market and in fashion to which

they may instantly react. Yet, the centralization at this level is in sharp contrast with the decentralization of manufacture. Less than 2,000 people are working at 8 plants in Northern Italy. Additionally, another 6,000 people are employed at 200 small-scale units outside the company. In this way overhead costs and wage costs are reduced as well as the opportunity for labourers to organize themselves. The number of Italian housewives willing to (or having to) work at home for an extremely low pay is sufficiently large".

Similar developments are also taking place in the Netherlands. Especially in the cities of Western Holland quite a few illegal clothing sweatshops are active. They are often producing articles for well-established companies such as C & A. A statement made by Mr De Koning, Minister for Social Services and Employment, proves that Dutch Government is well-informed on these developments. Early 1987 he said in an interview: "*Walk alongside the Amsterdam canals and do have a look at the basement flats. You will see Turkish women knocking together blouses at an hourly pay of Dfl. 3.50 to Dfl. 4.00* (Rs 20-25).

What is also significant is the trend towards industrial home-working among women; it has been growing considerably in Western Europe. Here again, it practically always concerns women and children doing manufacturing jobs in bad and unhealthy labour situations for extremely low wages and with no rights.

CONCLUSION: WILL THE MULTINATIONALS GO BACK TO THE INDUSTRIALISED WORLD?

In the previous section the historical development of the international division of labour has been reviewed. The three periods distinguished all have their own specific features. During the *colonial time* the colonies primarily supplied raw materials and agricultural produce and they were the outlets for goods manufactured in the colonial mother countries. Since the *mid-*

1960s the relation between developed and developing countries has undergone a qualitative change, which was affected by the *push and pull factors* as described above, and also enabled by rapid technological developments. A new international division of labour has emerged: the Third World countries have taken care of the labour-intensive branches, whereas companies with more advanced production technologies can be found in the West. Subsequently, the last section of this chapter dealt with the *latest developments*. Owing to economic crisis and technological advance, important changes occur again. The new restructuring within some industrial sectors both in the West and in the Third World lead to, amongst others, (international) subcontracting, growth of home-working and temporary employment contracts in the West.

For some industrial sectors and a great many companies the question whether it is still profitable to have (parts of) the production process take place in the Third World has become obtrusive. Labour costs in the West can be considerably reduced due to factors such as temporary employment contracts, home-working and subcontracting. Moreover, the latest *technological developments* have a great impact. For example, as a result of Japanese management techniques and far-reaching technological developments resulting in continuously advancing automation (e.g. computer-controlled equipment), companies in some sectors are in a position to manufacture at increasingly lower costs in the developed countries themselves. In the clothing industry, for instance, it is computers which are designing fashion nowadays, and laser beams which are cutting the fabrics. Thus, considerable reductions in labour costs emerge. Hence some people predict that "*in the long run the robot with its speed will outperform, amongst others, the Asian girls with their dexterity*". This way of reducing labour costs is doing away with some major advantages of setting up a company in the Third World.

Accordingly, the question proves to be justified: "*Will the multinationals go back to the industrialised world?*" It is too early yet to reply with a straightforward "yes", although it is true that the first clothing factories (especially those producing high-fashion articles) are on their way back to Western Europe. They had left this continent and passing North Africa (Tunesia), they went to the Far East (Taiwan, Malaysia and Hong Kong). Conversely, some Third World countries, for instance those in the Far East, are growing in significance as outlets, especially because more and more industrial buyers (of components of micro electronics, for instance) are concentrated in this area. On the other hand, in Western Europe, too, the purchasing power of a large part of the population is decreasing. Furthermore, a growing number of companies operating internationally tend to focus on *trading* goods and to put out the production to local entrepreneurs, who often get their hands tied to these companies.

We are still in the dark about what will precisely happen, and how, for it appears that there are different, sometimes opposite tendencies, which have different effects on various sectors and regions on earth. One thing is clear indeed, international firms will continue to shift jobs from one place to another as long as they have not found that location where they can produce at the lowest possible costs.

Selected Bibliography

P. Dicken, *Global shift; Industrial change in a turbulent world*, Londen (Harper & Row), 1986.

R. Palme Dutt, *India To-day*, Bombay (Manisha), 1979.

F.F. Clairmonte en J. Cavanagh, Global economic debacle and corporate power, *Economic and Political Weekly*, March 28, 1987, pp. 559-563.

F. Fröbel, J. Heinrichs en O. Kreye, *The new international division of labour: structural unemployment in the industrial countries and industrialisation in developing countries*, Cambridge (Cambridge Univ. Press), 1980.

A. Fuentes en B. Ehrenreich, *Women in the global factory*, Boston (South End Press), 1984.

S. Lall en P. Streeten, *Foreign investment, transnationals and developing countries*, London (Macmillan Press), 1977.

N. Lucas, Internationale arbeidsverdeling en vrouwenarbeid: enkele nieuwe ontwikkelingen (International division of labour and womens' work: some recent trends), *Tijdschrift voor politieke ekonomie*, nr. 1, 1985, pp. 101-115.

M. Mies, *Patriarchy and accumulation on a world scale; Women in the international division of labour*, London (Zed Books), 1986.

S. Mitter, *Common fate, common bond; Women in the global economy*, London (Pluto Press), 1986.

The Fortune 500 largest US industrial corporations, *Fortune*, April 27, 1987.

United Nations Centre on Transnational Corporations (UNCTC), *Transnational Corporations in world development; Third Survey*, New York (United Nations), 1983.

F. van der Velden, *Ontwikkelingssamenwerking vanuit West-Europa met India; Drie case-studies (Development cooperation from Western Europe with India; Three case-studies)*, Nijmegen (Derde Wereld Centrum), 1980.

F. van der Velden, *Ancillarisation by subsidiaries of Dutch companies in India; Is small beautiful?*, New Delhi/Nijmegen, (to be published).

Chapter 2

INTERNATIONAL RESTRUCTURING OF EMPLOYMENT AT A REGIONAL LEVEL

Ger van den Broek

For many regions in Western Europe employment is increasingly being affected by international developments. In this article the patterns and processes of international restructuring and the role of international firms are considered at a regional level and illustrated by an example of a region in the Netherlands: Nijmegen and environs. Dubbed "Europe's Silicon Valley" in the international press, Nijmegen is a region in which multinational corporations lend a substantial contribution to employment. Nevertheless, judged by Dutch as well as West European standards it has to contend with an extremely high unemployment rate.

EMPLOYMENT AND REGIONAL DEVELOPMENT

By January 1987 the number of unemployed registered in the Nijmegen region was nearly 25,000. This is equivalent to 26 percent of the labour force (men 23 percent, women well over 30 percent). In spite of the fact that in recent years regional business has experienced economic prosperity, a drop in the unemployment rate has not been reported yet. In recent years the growth in jobs has just been sufficient to meet the annual increase in the working population. In December 1986 it was anticipated that unemployment would stabilize at about 25,500 in 1987, which implied that in 1987 again the unemployment rate of this region was likely to be higher than that of all other regions in the Netherlands. Even a further rise in unemployment among women was expected.

Regarding the growth in jobs, it should be noted that in particular the number of *part-time* jobs is booming. The rise in full-time jobs remains at a much lower level; for one reason, this is due to the fact that full-time employment is being split up into part-time jobs. By now well over half of the positions occupied by women are part-time. Owing to the growth in part-time employment and the *reduction of working hours*, the development of the *labour volume* (the amount of work expressed in manyears) has been lagging behind the *number of jobs* considerably ever since 1980. As a result the growth rate figures of regional employment, especially those of women, are misleading. Additionally, the first half of the 1980s witnessed a much steeper drop in employment than is suggested by the development in the number of jobs. For the Arnhem-Nijmegen region the decrease in the number of jobs over the 1980-1984 period was estimated at 7 percent while the labour volume soared by an estimated 12 percent. In this period the number of part-time jobs rose by 16 percent, whereas, according to the same estimate, the number of full-time jobs fell by 13 percent.

The recent process of redivision of labour is less and less realized by the reduction of working hours (less working hours a week/year with full or partial recomplement), but more and more it is effected by a growth in part-time jobs and *temporary* employment contracts. As policy aims, particularly those of the labour unions, are playing an important role in the demand of reduction of working hours (shorter working weeks as an instrument for reducing unemployment), recent developments are mainly a reflection of the changing demands of employers on their personnel. In this process the redivision of labour occurs at the most as an additional effect. These shifts are often placed under the heading "*making labour flexible*" (see chapter 1 for this). For one thing, the growing supply of part-time jobs may hold opportunities for paid jobs for more people in search of employment and lead to sharing the breadwinner's role. For another, the statement may be made that although part-time jobs are artificially holding down the unemployment figures in the official statistics, in general this does not yet provide prosperity. The growth in part-time work, temporary contracts, on-call contracts, home-working etc. is accompanied by an increase in low wages (often below the basic unemployment benefit level), more insecurity, less prospects (concerning promotion or career development) and as a result, poor legal status with respect to social provisions and regulations as laid down in collective labour agreements. As a result the quality of employment offered is deteriorating, especially for young people, migrants and women.

For years now, in fact, even before World War II the unemployment rate in Nijmegen has been considerably higher than the national average, specifically in times of economic crises as was the case during the depression of the 1930s and in the early 1950s. From 1975 onwards the unemployment rate has been at a level of twice the national average.

Therefore, today's unemployment is not entirely due to recent developments. A major cause is found in the weak structure, slow progress and the small volume of employment in Nijmegen and environs. These related issues are the theme of this article. It focuses upon the regional *industry*, in which the total number of jobs has been cut by more than half over the last few decades.

In order to find an explanation for this weak and one-sided development, it is essential to have an understanding of the regional development process. In this article regional development is taken to be a process of continuous conflict between the *locational demands* made by firms and the *production conditions* offered by regions. Locational demands as well as production conditions are subject to continuous change and they all have their own specific development patterns. Expansion of particular activities in the form of so-called investment rounds is feasible when the locational demands and the production conditions correspond during a particular period (e.g. the demand for a great many low-skilled workers and a large supply of them). As a consequence, regional economic expansion is a *selective* growth process which at any particular time may involve various different parts of the regional economy. This is the reason why even between regions the extent in which employment is affected by changes in economic development may show considerable difference. In a more general sense the regional development over the last few decades may be considered a conflict between the restructuring of manufacture at a global level and the historical growth of regional development conditions. The latter includes the specific manufacturing structure (specializations), infrastructure, the presence of particular raw materials, (alterations in) location, quality and size of the working population, labour reserve etc. International restructuring processes specifically reveal themselves in the regions through investment decisions taken by multinational corporations in particular as a reaction to trends in the market, technology and the organization of manufacture.

LITTLE INDUSTRY OF OLD

Compared to several other Dutch cities, industrial development in Nijmegen had an extremely late start. Till the close of the previous century Nijmegen was a fortified city lying enclosed within the town ramparts; lack of space limited the introduction and expansion of new industrial activities. Building was prohibited right outside the ramparts. The limited number of industrial and especially traditional entrepreneurs were reluctant to welcome competitors from elsewhere. This was, amongst other things, due to the fact that manufacture and, of course, trades were principally regional services. For years the emergent middle classes had attacked the constraints of Nijmegen's status as a fortified city, however, strong industrial expansion failed to occur even after the dismantlement of the ramparts, which had been started in 1874. Most of all the building industry was expanding. Furthermore, some growth was seen in the sectors providing vital necessities such as the clothing and food industries.

The local authorities in the previous century regarded Nijmegen, first of all, as an attractive *residential town* which, for example, was apparent in the preference held by repatriates from the then Dutch East Indies for taking up their residence in Nijmegen and environs when they returned, and from the appeal of the city as a holiday resort. The presence of many well-to-do pensioners and *people living off their interests*, who put a conservative influence on the local authorities, yielded a nickname for the city: *pensionopolis*. Moreover, this reinforced services as the central characteristic of employment. In 1899 approximately one-fifth of the working population was still working in the so-called "domestic services".

The pursuit of industrialisation did not fit into this picture. Large factories, specifically heavy industry and the means of production industries which might give an impetus to other branches, stayed away from Nijmegen. There is no doubt that the isolated location of the Nijmegen region, which was reinforced by increased development towards the west of the Netherlands into an economic centre and the declining significance of river transport, added to this late and slow development. It was not until the turn of the century that some industry of consequence expanded into Nijmegen, such as nuts and bolts, transformers, and detergent factories as well as some textile factories. Owing to the electrification of urban and rural areas, some light bulb factories emerged, however, most of them tasted defeat after a brief period of growth, particularly because of a much more successful, rapidly expanding competitor, *Philips*, from the south of the Netherlands, which became one of the world's leading bulb producers in a short time.

Areas surrounding the city of Nijmegen such as the "*Land van Maas en Waal*", also faced a late and slow industrial development. Its development was confined to the emergence of some brick and tile factories, a number of shipyards along the river Waal and some small local dairy factories. After World War II a modest furniture industry emerged, initially as a subsidiary of the shipbuilding industry present in the area.

The period around the turn of the century shows that in Europe activities were more and more being concentrated in the hands of large enterprises (and monopolies) and the orientation towards expanding *world markets* was increasing. The colonies, growing in number and significance, played a major role in this process, especially those supplying raw materials (see chapter 1). In the Netherlands the acceleration of the industrialisation process took place specifically in the western part of the country, where production conditions were most favourable for big companies and for the so-called world market industries in particular. Although in the first decades of this century industrial growth was also reported in Nijmegen and environs, the region was lagging behind the strong expansion and concentration in the west of the country. Typically, Nijmegen was not involved in the introduction of large-scale industry, which was especially dominant in the period after 1914. By 1930 still no enterprises employing over 1,000 people had settled in this area. It was only later that *Kunstzijde Spinnerij Nyma*, an artificial silk spinning mill, had a labour force of that size. In 1930 the 45-percent proportion of the working population in industry (building, manufacture and trades) was considerably smaller than that of typical industrial cities in eastern and southern parts of the Netherlands, such as Eindhoven, Enschede and Tilburg, where it was approximately 70 percent. It was not until this century that activities which had developed in these and a host of other cities as early as the nineteenth century, such as the textile and leather industries, were substantially growing in Nijmegen. Moreover, the relative size of the total working population was markedly below the level of most other cities.

Figures from a company-and-occupation count in 1930 revealed that the number of workers leaving Nijmegen daily was greater than those entering. Certainly at that time this was an odd phenomenon for a city of its size, from which the inference may be drawn that Nijmegen was incapable of acting as a centre of employment for an extensive surrounding area. Even after 1900 attention was repeatedly being drawn to its slow industrial development, specifically by the *Kamer van Koophandel*, (the body responsible for the registration of businesses). Planned industrial projects, such as large industrial estates and a new port on the river however, could not be realized before World War II. Consequently, during the depression of the 1930s the unemployment rate was exceptionally high in Nijmegen.

REBUILDING AND ECONOMIC GROWTH

Only after World War II, industrialisation was actually getting off the ground. Vigorous economic growth on an international as well as a national level was beneficial to the region. And, with some specific advantages, Nijmegen had a selective appeal to companies intent on settling in the area. At that time it was one of the Dutch regions with relative low wages and a vast supply of labour. Moreover, the Nijmegen population were not generally militant, which was, amongst other things, due to the lack of an industrial tradition as had arisen in other parts of the Netherlands. The lack of a firm industrial base, however, precluded the emergence of a varied and strong economic structure. At first, industrial growth was taking place partially in the labour-intensive sectors which had developed in the decades before the war. With respect to Dutch economy as a whole, they were already past their peak. This was particularly the case for the textile, clothing and footwear industries, which had numerous new plants soon after the war, but whose vulnerability came to light as early as the beginning of the 1960s. From the mid-1950s the growth rates of these sectors have fallen. A sharp increase in employment has been experienced in the metal industry and electrical engineering, in which from 1965 up till today well over half the employment in manufacture has been concentrated. The restructuring processes in this sector will be dealt with later in this article.

In the "*Land van Maas en Waal*" development did not go beyond the expansion of the limited industrial activities already existing. At first rebuilding and the population boom were of great benefit to business, specifically to brick and tile manufacturers and the furniture industry. There was just one new company of some significance, *Hendrix' Vlees* at Druten, which was founded in 1974 by Hendrix' Veevoederfabrieken (Hendrix' Feed Factories). Their key motive for settling was the presence of pig farms in this area. Hendrix is a booming concern operating internationally, which was taken over in 1979 by *British Petroleum*, second on the list, after Shell, of the largest non-American enterprises in the world.

RETRIBUTION FOR ONE-SIDEDNESS

In the mid-1950s the textile, clothing and footwear industries accounted for a good 35 percent of employment in the Nijmegen manufacturing industry. The most of the now disappeared companies employed at least some hundreds of people each. At the beginning of the 1960s Nyma, the artificial silk spinning mill employed as many as 1,200 people, of which only less than 100 have remained. In 1967 Swift, a Nijmegen ladies' footwear plant and Robinson, a men's footwear plant, merged. The outcome was the largest footwear plant in the Netherlands employing almost 1,000 people. Since then, contraction followed upon contraction until in 1981 the company went bankrupt. The year of 1969 gave a foretaste of what would recur several times again. Nyma closed down her artificial silk spinning mill making 750 people redundant at one go. Only the company's chemistry department has remained. Still, there was a significant difference with the present situation. In less than a year *De Gelderlander*, the regional daily, reported that nearly all former Nyma workers had found another job.

Since 1965 the size of the textile and leather industry in the Nijmegen region has decreased by approximately 90 percent. Various other sectors such as clothing, metal products and machinery were cut by more than half. Also in other parts of the Netherlands employment in these sectors was rapidly declining. Yet Nijmegen reported more redundancies and close-downs than other areas, which was due to an overrepresentation of these sectors in this area. Whereas in the 1965-1980 period employment in manufacture in the Netherlands soared by 17 percent, the Nijmegen region reported a drop of approximately 40 percent. Large parts of, amongst others, textile and clothing industry, but also footwear industry, were transferred to South European and Third World countries with a sizable labour supply and a low pay rate: i.e. *the low-wage countries*. Additionally, this led to a worsening of the competitive position of the "backward" enterprises in these branches. Some factors which may account for the international restructuring of these labour-intensive branches are: the internationalization of several previously Dutch textile and clothing enterprises, the sharp rise in wages in the Netherlands in the mid-1960s after a period of tightly controlled wage policies, and the scarcity of labour. In the Nijmegen region, too, unemployment was negligible, while simultaneously so-called guestworkers were mobilized in the manufacturing process. In the first chapter the general backgrounds of this international shift were dealt with extensively implying the factors acting on it from Third World countries.

NEW DEPENDENCY

In addition to sectorial shifts generated by international restructuring processes, another related trend has also emerged since the mid-1960s bringing about a significant change in the character of regional economy. More and more international firms with foreign as well as Dutch roots, and national companies, set up branches or subsidiaries in the Nijmegen area. What's more, a considerable number of independent Nijmegen companies were taken over in the course of time. This is the reason why industrialisation of the Nijmegen region, which got well under way only after World War II, was primarily realized by investments and initiatives from outside.

At first, mainly *American* multinationals were involved, which, in comparison with European enterprises, had switched over to internationalization at a much earlier stage. The majority of American enterprises started off on a better footing than their competitors on the European continent, which suffered the aftereffects of war. *Friden* (later Singer) *CC Controls* (a Singer subsidiary, too), *Hyster*, *Coleman* and *Heinz* set up new plants in the Nijmegen region, and a rapid growth in employment resulted. Activities of these new American plants could generally be classified as mass production of matured goods, partly manufactured under licence. They usually involved routine assembly activities in the metal industry and electrical engineering. In some cases the Netherlands was chosen as the location for production with an eye to its function as a stepping stone to the European market. In the Netherlands themselves Nijmegen was particularly popular because of its relatively large supply of low-skilled labourers, low pay rates and a low level of social tensions and industrial disputes.

In 1953 *Philips* also settled in Nijmegen. Those were the years during which Philips, having grown into an international firm even before the war, radiated from Eindhoven throughout the Netherlands. The spreading policy carried through by the top management of the company resulted after a while in 70 plants located at 70 places in the Netherlands. Its target work force was young, low-skilled labourers in the peripheral problem areas of the northern, southern and eastern parts of the Netherlands. Compared to the present character of the Nijmegen Philips plant, employment throughout the 1950s and 1960s was characterized by a strong emphasis on direct manufacture and relatively labour-intensive routine assembly activities. At that time relatively many young women were involved in the Philips production activities. In the course of time the work they did disappeared as a consequence of automation and product innovations or it was transferred to low-wage countries: i.e. to Southeast Asian plants with which Philips has maintained strong production relations up till the present day.

From the mid-1960s there was a substantial introduction of *European* (including Dutch) multinationals and other Dutch firms into the region. Examples of Dutch firms and multinationals are *KNP, AKZO, Holec, DSM, Shell, Wessanen* and *Meneba.* Several European firms also started operating in the Nijmegen region. Amongst them were *AML-Distibutors, BOC, British Petroleum* and *Rowntree Macintosh,* all British, *Rustfri* from Denmark, *Cockerill* from Belgium and *Hoesch, Vaillant* and *Veba,* all West German multinationals. Finally, the American *IMC* took over the considerably reduced Nyma plant.

In contrast to the 1950s, nearly all cases involved the *take-over* of existing firms. Compared to the previous period, the role of American enterprises was modest. Throughout this period the increasing number of international firms in the Nijmegen region was no longer accompanied by growing employment. All the same, the outcome of this development was that in the mid-1970s subsidiaries of firms operating internationally accounted for over two-thirds of employment in manufacturing industries. In 1975 over 7,000 jobs, that is, 60 percent of the manufacturing jobs in the city of Nijmegen, were to be found in a mere 7 multinational enterprises: *AKZO, Hyster, Singer,* (2 plants in Nijmegen), *Holec* (4), *KNP, KSH* (2) and *Philips* (2). This intensified the vulnerability of the industrial sector, weak as it already was. The implication was that decisions concerning expansion, contraction, investments and jobs were increasingly being determined abroad or elsewhere in the Netherlands. Moreover, first priority in decision-making was no longer given to the interests of the Nijmegen-based company but to those of the entire corporation. The developments at *Hyster,* manufacturer of forklifts, show how company interests can be translated into global shifts in manufacture and employment. Assuming that manufacturing should take place at the location with the lowest possible production costs, the American management of this company mounted a full-scale international reorganization in the early 1980s. Appeals for financial help to the various countries and American states where Hyster plants were located were invariably accompanied by threats of closure if no sufficient financial support was forthcoming. In the case of the Scottish Hyster plant the workers were pressurized to such an extent that they accepted a 15-percent pay reduction in exchange for keeping their jobs. Owing to employee and labour union action, plans to progressively reduce production in Nijmegen could be checked, however, still 165 jobs were lost. These events showed how such a restructuring allowed international firms to build a strong position of power in which they divided official bodies and employees in various countries and regions and played them off against each other as competitors.

The drive for expansion and the pursuit of *diversification* figured largely in the take-overs mentioned above. The process was promoted by the creation and the development of the European Community, as a result of which easier access was gained to the relatively protectionist national markets in Western Europe. But above all things, the realization of an expanded Western European market resulted in strong *consolidation tendencies* mainly involving European multinationals. In the 1970s such tendencies were intensified when the growth of markets began to stagnate and enterprises switched over to keeping their market shares or, alternatively enlarging them after all by taking over and eliminating their competitors. Consolidation processes were manifest in two ways. *Firstly*, they revealed themselves at an enterprise level: small-size (national) companies and independent enterprises were absorbed into a larger business structure. Take-overs were not restricted to companies operating in the same branch. In the 1960s and 1970s various international firms pursued a diversification strategy which was realized by purchasing businesses foreign to the branch itself. For example, *British Petroleum* took over the Hendrix' concern, which included Hendrix' Vlees Druten, and *Holec* purchased the Nijmegen *Smit* Companies.

Secondly, consolidation occurred at a geographical level, which affected different regions to a varying extent. Usually, the productive activities of the companies taken over were amalgated with the production of the business they merged into: they were adopted to efficient, large-scale locations, which had the most favourable conditions for production. For the most part these were existing (larger) plants of the concern, located elsewhere. For the Nijmegen region the effects of this process were mainly negative, which was due to the transfer of production, know-how and, sometimes, labour to locations outside the region. In the 1970s in particular, various Dutch and foreign enterprises bought companies in this region and closed them down or sold them (stripped) within one or a few more years. This was a major cause of the surge of closures and contractions of companies and the redundancies associated with it. An appreciation that the Nijmegen region had been hit very hard indeed gave rise to the development of the "*Aktieplan Werkgelegenheid*" (Action Programme for Job Opportunities), a local movement consisting of labour unions, environmental groups, women's groups, groups representing the interests of small-scale firms and various social groups. The Aktieplan drew attention primarily because it offered alternatives to the (threat of) redundancies for subsidiaries of international firms through so-called employees' programmes which, in some cases, could successfully offset the disinvestment strategies adopted by a number of businesses operating in Nijmegen.

RECENT DEVELOPMENTS

With the economic crisis getting more severe, the activities of European multinationals in the region were lapsing in the early 1980s. The number of subsidiaries of international firms was also falling, which was a consequence of the scrapping or closing down of the uneconomic activities of the corporations, the gaining independence of companies as a result of the disintegration of corporations and the withdrawal of parent companies to core activities as a reaction to the past diversification which had been pushed (too) far.

A decade ago the Smit companies, originally Nijmegen-based and by the end of the 1960s largely taken over by the *Holec* corporation, still had a labour force of about 1,500 people. Since then, reorganization has followed upon reorganization causing the loss of hundreds of jobs. Some of the Nijmegen-based parts of the firm (a factory turning out industrial ovens, another welding electrodes, one producing large transformers and a thread factory) were partly or entirely scrapped because they were said to be no longer fitting in the range of Holec activities. Of what used to be the Nijmegen Holec bastion just one company entirely controlled by the corporation is left, employing about one hundred people, and a 50-percent stake in the rigorously reduced factory of large transformers. *Nyma*, mentioned before, became an independent company again. In 1982 *CC Controls* (bankrupt in the meantime) came back into Dutch hands after the disintegration of its Danish parent company. Dividing the *Estel* corporation meant that the head office of this German-Dutch steel giant was no longer based in Nijmegen.

In the 1980s however, this region has simultaneously experienced an increase in plants owned by American enterprises. Just as in the 1950s, this expansion has come about mainly by *setting up* new plants. Some newly-emerged American multinationals (*Sealed Air, Printronix*) have set up their first European plants in Nijmegen, as stepping stones to the West European market. Other American firms which have come to this region since 1980, are *Borden, Bristol Myers* and *Intergraph*. The *Canadian Development Corporation* took over *Daisy Systems* from the Dutch State.

The table below presents a survey of the share of international firms in manufacturing jobs in the Nijmegen region in 1985. In some sectors employment is concentrated for two-thirds or more in the hands of subsidiaries of these firms. In these sectors, trends in employment are thus greatly dependent on the investment strategies of a very limited number of international enterprises whether of foreign or Dutch origin.

Share of international firms in employment in manufacturing in the Nijmegen region (1985)

	International firms		Number of jobs in all companies[2]
	Number of companies	Share in percentages	
Total industy	23	49[1]	15,070
including			
food and kindred industries	6	67	2,320
building materials and the like	2	23	750
paper industry	1	90	650
chemicals	4	36	800
metal industry and electrical engineering[3]	10	64	7,230
other industries	0	0	3,320

1. For the city of Nijmegen this is 61 percent (estimate). Other employment can be found in national Dutch companies and independent enterprises in the region. Percentages in this column are estimates based on statements provided by the companies themselves, Chamber of Commerce and various other sources.
2. As stated in the Provincial Employment Questionnaire.
3. Including basic metal, fabricated metal products, machinery, electrical engineering, transport equipment and instruments engineering.

SHIFTS IN MANUFACTURING STRUCTURE

The development of the regional manufacturing structure has been accompanied by the loss of activities in which this region used to be specialized. Broadly speaking, *three stages* can be distinguished in this process, which may summarize the developments described in this chapter. These three partly overlapping stages of industrial progress run parallel with the emergence and expansion of another three groups of industrial activities, which have subsequently left their mark on the development of employment.

Firstly, strong restructuring processes showing themselves in substantial losses in employment, took place within industrial activities which had grown as early as the second half of the previous century. Activities such as the building materials industry, shipbuilding and repairs and parts of the food, drink and tabacco industry (specifically dairy) emerged primarily based on then existing locational advantages, such as being situated on the river, the presence of raw materials and local/regional outlets. During the last few decades the dairy industry has almost disappeared from the region; in the 1975-1985 period employment in the manufacture of building materials was cut by a good 50 percent while in the same period the regional shipbuilding and repair industry also suffered heavy job losses.

Secondly, it concerned labour-intensive activities which developed only later, after World War II, such as the textile, clothing and leather industries; in the "Land van Maas en Waal" it was especially the wood and furniture industry. Previously, even before 1900, the clothing industry and trade had grown servicing the local Nijmegen market. In the course of the nineteenth century textile industry, too, had become important. The focus was more and more shifted towards national and international markets. A major factor featuring in this trend was the large supply of cheap low and unskilled labour as a result of, amongst other things, heavy job losses in agriculture. Since the late 1960s losses in employment have become extremely severe, which may be attributed to the international restructuring processes outlined earlier in this chapter. They led to an almost complete disappearance of these activities from the region.

A *third* group of activities, restructured to a great extent during the crisis which had set in since the 1970s, is made up by the regional metal industry and electrical engineering. Though parts of the metal industry had developed even before that, metal and electronics have boomed in Nijmegen and environs since the 1950s. The development mainly involved plants of foreign and Dutch corporations. Most of the companies focused on assembly activities of fully matured mass production from elsewhere. Throughout the 1970s various companies were facing problems: *commodities* were largely getting *out of date* whereas product innovation, due to the character of the subsidiaries in this region as previously mentioned, was taking place in other parts of the firm, located elsewhere. Substantial parts of the region's metal industry and electrical engineering were subject to accelerated recession, because economic crisis reinforced stagnation of the companies' markets. As a consequence of the sharp reduction in capacity, the scrapping of parts of manufacture and close-downs, the restructuring process went hand in hand with a massive loss of labour. Additionally, owing to the lapse in returns in various companies, a *cost reduction* strategy was emphasized as a result of which staffing was reduced to a level of bare necessity.

In 1975 the city of Nijmegen counted still 6 companies operating in the metal industry and electrical engineering each employing over 500 people. By 1985, only *Philips* Nijmegen, which had realized a considerable growth in employment, still retained a labour force larger than that. Due to contractions and close-downs, the other five (all subsidiaries including *Singer* and *Hyster*), lost approximately 2,100 of the 3,600 jobs during this period. The two next largest enterprises in this sector in 1975 (both having a labour force of between 400 and 500 people) were closed down. Recently, employment in the regional metal industry and electrical engineering has witnessed a slight increase again, for the first time in years. To a great extent recent growth is the result of the fact that already existing production capacities were taken into production again, which was made possible by a strong market recovery. New foreign plants and product innovation, especially at *Philips*, have also fuelled a rise in employment.

The diagram below shows the trends in employment in the city of Nijmegen this century for some industrial activities, which each was or has been essential for a particular stage of regional development. It becomes evident that the conflict between the region's ever-changing *advantages* over decades and the *demands* of the enterprises has led to a shift in industrial activities. This is merely an indication, for the nature of the three groups of activities has obviously changed throughout this century (e.g. from a food industry geared to local service and based on local raw materials to specialized production by multinationals servicing the world markets and based on raw materials and semiproducts which are partly imported). Nevertheless, the pattern of regional development described can easily be identified.

Development of some industrial activities in the city of Nijmegen since 1900 (jobs in thousands)

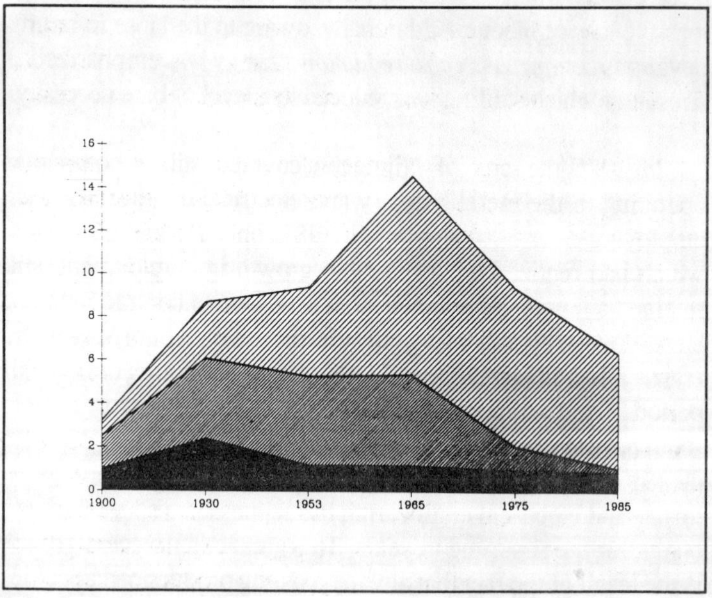

food and kindred industries
textile, clothing and leather industries
metal industry and electrical engineering

Locational factors that can account for the arrival of the aforementioned enterprises have partly declined in significance. This has applied most, and even for long time, to the natural locational advantages mentioned. The region's relatively low pay rate has also become less important since the differences in pay in the Netherlands have greatly decreased. Nevertheless, in some sectors such as the metal industry and electrical engineering they have still not completely disappeared. Additionally, the favourable working climate and the almost total lack of social tensions and industrial disputes can less and less be deemed locational advantages specific to the region. On the other hand, the relatively large supply of (suitable) workers has remained over the last few decades. This factor seems to have come into play recently in the settling of some subsidiaries owned by American multinational corporations in particular. It is true that in Nijmegen especially some categories of highly qualified staff in technical posts, are facing bottlenecks. Yet this is not a specific Nijmegen problem: for this kind of jobs the labour market has no regional but a national or even international dimension. In the last few years its situation with respect to the European market has improved. This is a matter of interest, for investments in manufacture of international firms in the Netherlands have shown a shift from western to southern and eastern parts of the country in order to place the European market within good reach. Recent company investments, which for the first time in decades have fuelled a slight growth of jobs in manufacture, have also been affected by the extremely high investment grants obtainable in the Nijmegen area and surroundings.

To a considerable extent, the recent expansion in industry can be attributed to *Philips*, an enterprise which in a few years time has realized a rise in employment by 1,000 jobs and has become the biggest producer of ICs (chips) in Western Europe. The arrival of some American firms such as *Printronix, Digital* and *Intergraph* meant a further growth of micro-electronic activity. In contrast to what has been suggested, the integration of these companies into the regional economy has been insignificant so far. Furthermore, the companies mentioned have maintained no significant mutual production relations.

This also touches upon one of the salient features of the whole post-war industrial development in the Nijmegen region. In this period international firms were creating and destroying jobs, and additionally they were leaving their mark on the development of regional economy to an increasing extent. The high unemployment rate in the Nijmegen region cannot be directly attributed to the activities of international firms present in this area. Moreover, this would be too narrow an interpretation because it is not possible to isolate the developments in a single region from those in the outside world. The statement may be made however, that the continuing process of internationalization of industrial life and the increasing influence of international firms have placed more and more emphasis on including the Nijmegen region in international restructuring processes. Furthermore, due to its economic structure and (historical) development, this region has proved to be extremely vulnerable to the effects of these developments. Summarizing, four issues that came up in this article can be pointed out.

The transfer of labour to so-called low-wage countries in the 1960s and 1970s, taking place within the labour-intensive industries which used to be amply represented in this area, such as the clothing, textile, footwear and electrical industry.

Redundancies in the same period as a result of the fact that the range of products of some subsidiaries of international firms became more and more outdated, whereas new developments were realized in other parts of the firm located elsewhere.

The activities of most international firms located in the Nijmegen region during the postwar period gave little impetus to the development of other economic activities in manufacturing or elsewhere. This may be one of the reasons for the fact that the development of business services in Nijmegen and environs was lagging behind during this period.

THE ACQUISITION PROGRAMME OF THE CITY OF NIJMEGEN

The above mentioned investment grants are a fundamental pillar of the acquisition programme adopted by the city of Nijmegen in the 1980s. The aim of these grants is to attract multinational companies, especially from abroad. Under certain conditions the national Government pays for 35 percent of the investment costs of an enterprise expanding or setting up in the Nijmegen region. This is under the terms of the so-called *Investerings Premie Regeling* (I.P.R., that is, the Investment Grant Programme); this is in addition to grants generally obtainable as part of the *Wet Investerings Rekening* (W.I.R., that is, the Investment Account Act). Besides so-called "mailing" campaigns and promotion trips to the United States and Japan, the efforts of the local authorities consist of taking prompt and efficient action with regard to procedures and licences and offering other facilities ranging from reduced prices of land, housing for staff members who are relocated, to moving a road. An acquisition programme as pursued by the city of Nijmegen for instance, is not in the last place a reflection of increased competition between regions at home and abroad. This is illustrated by the increasing advertising efforts of many regions in Western Europe in the national and international press. Choosing a perspective transcending the scope of a single region one sees that the main concern of this acquisition programme is not with creating jobs but merely with manipulating the place where employment should be located. In cases in which, with a special 35 percent government grant for investment (from the IPR kitty) and additional support from the local authorities, the mere achievement is that an enterprise stays away from another deprived region, this kind of regional employment programme is an expensive and inefficient system. It was expensive, for example, when the government grant for the Bristol Myers Corporation plant, opened in 1985, amounted to hundreds of thousands of guilders per job. Within the more limited scope of the local authorities in whose policies local/regional issues are priority, this acquisition programme is considered a successful example of the region's economic development programme. For the local authorities the costs of this programme turn out to be quite reasonable, for it is easy to take advantage of the IPR and WIR grants, paid for by the national Government. Estimates of the employment effects of this programme vary, depending on whether the role of the municipal system resulting in the eventual arrival of companies is considered decisive, whether or not the relocation of staff members associated with the move are taken into account, etc.

The acquisition programme is chiefly a *selling* policy. To create an attractive reputation for the region exaggerated terms have been adopted such as, *Nijmegen, Europe's Silicon Valley, the high-tech* character of the activities already attracted, *structural reinforcement* as a result of the arrival of new international firms and Nijmegen as a *Burgundian business centre*. The council paper "*Nijmegen on the market, the city's economic programme of 1986-1989*" links up with this: "*As far as the reputation of the city (region) is concerned it should be noted that in economic respects Nijmegen is not a deprived city (region). There are clear indications that "weeping and wailing" and pigeonholing oneself are counterproductive and likely to deter investors*".

Furthermore, this quotation and the title of this paper mark a shift from a policy aimed at employment to a programme concerned with economic structure. The same paper states that the effects of the economic programme "*will be of relatively little significance*" for the growing hard core of long-term unemployed.

It is impossible to imagine the regional economy without multinational corporations. They account for an estimated 60 percent of employment in the city of Nijmegen (1985). The acquisition of international firms generates a further increase in dependency on the strategies of these enterprises. The resulting increased vulnerability has also been recognized by the Nijmegen city council. It is associated with the specific function of subsidiaries in regions such as Nijmegen within the international firms they are part of. The nature of manufacture (repair and distribution) activities of these subsidiaries, which was described earlier in this chapter, had a large impact on this function. A matter of interest is, for example, that backward and forward linkages of these subsidiaries are for the most part within the firm, that is, outside the region. This implies that the effects on employment in the region are limited. In exchange for enormous amounts of financial support more could be demanded of international firms in this respect. Strong dominance of international firms over regional economy raises of few questions concerning the aims of the city's acquisition programme affecting the region's economy as well as its employment. How can other enterprises, independent companies and small and medium-sized business be stimulated in acting as suppliers of goods and services without becoming overdependent on one or few buyers by introducing multinational corporations into the region? How can an actual structural reinforcement through encouraging collaboration between existing small and medium-sized businesses result in more jobs?

Selected bibliography

Ben Alders, Ger van den Broek en Marcel Meijs, *Het dochterbedrijf Nijmegen BV; Multinationale ondernemingen en de industriële werkgelegenheid in Nijmegen*, Nijmegen, 1982.

Ger van den Broek en Marcel Meijs, *Werkgelegenheid en Werkloosheid in Midden-Gelderland; herstrukturering van het bedrijfsleven sinds 1975*, Nijmegen (Wetenschapswinkel i.s.m. Economisch Instituut), 1987.

Fred Crone en Henk Overbeek (ed.), *Nederlands kapitaal over de grenzen*, Amsterdam (SUA), 1981.

Mike Danson (ed.), *Redundancy and recession: restructuring the region?*, Norwich (Geo Books), 1986.

Michael Dunford, Mike Geddes , Diane Perrons, Regional Policy and the crisis in the U.K.: a long run perspective. *International Journal of Urban and Regional Research*, nr. 2, 1981, pp. 377-411.

A. Loeve, Buitenlandse ondernemingen in Nederland, *Economisch Statistische Berichten*, 26 februari 1986, pp. 220-226.

Dieter Läpple en Jan Laurier, *De ruimtelijke gevolgen van economische struktuurveranderingen*, Leiden (Onderzoekscentrum Ruimtelijke Ontwikkeling en Volkshuisvesting R.U.L.), 1986.

Doreen Massey en Richard Meegan, *The anatomy of Job Loss; The how, why and where of employment decline*, Londen (Methuen), 1982.

Werner Mikus, Regional Concentration in Multiplant Enterprises, *Geo Journal*, vol. 9, no. 2, 1984, pp. 105-110.

W.B. Stöhr, Regional economic development and the world economic crisis, *International Social Science Journal*, nr. 112, 1987, pp. 187-199.

A.R. Towsend and F.W. Peck, The geography of mass-redundancy in named corporations, in: M. Pacione (ed.), *Progress in industrial geography*, London (Croom Helm), 1985.

J. de Vries, *Nieuw Nijmegen, 1870-1970, Moderne economische geschiedenis van de stad Nijmegen*, Tilburg, 1969.

Chapter 3

CASES TO ANSWER: SUBSIDIARIES OF MULTINATIONALS IN THE NIJMEGEN REGION

compiled by Lau Schulpen

INTRODUCTION

In this chapter we want to illustrate what kind of effects investment decisions taken by multinational corporations have on the economic structure and employment in a region. Our examples are firms from Nijmegen and its surrounding area, operating in various sectors of the manufacturing industries. Each of them highlights different aspects of the new international division of labour and points to the (rather limited) role of Nijmegen's city council in attracting and controlling industry. Moreover, they give an idea of the difficulties and obstacles labour unions have to face when dealing with firms operating internationally.

These cases are by no means representative of all aspects of international economy nor of all the effects within the Nijmegen region, but they do shed some light on a number of trends.

MacIntosh, working in the clothing sector, is a good example of how investment patterns are affected by relatively high labour costs. In this case it resulted in a complete dismantling of the trade in Nijmegen. Ironically, in the end the firm came back as a trader and is now selling its "world products" under a different name.

The interesting aspect of the example of Philips is the relation between technological developments and the consequent transfer of parts of the production process to other countries. Moreover, access to newly-developed markets seems to play a decisive role in the strategy of this firm from the electronics sector.

One of the smaller multinational firms in the Netherlands, operating in the field of agrobusiness, is Nutricia. The history of this firm is illustrative of the way in which a firm that used to be nationally-oriented becomes (or is forced to become) multinational; in this case by merging with Cow & Gate _ and thereby with Unigate.

The part on Hyster focuses on the conflicts between firms and labour unions as well as between firms and city councils or national governments, and on the resulting struggle for job and investment control. Labour unionists all over the world will probably recognize some of their own experiences in this example.

Bristol Myers, a company which has become notorious for the use of baby food in Third World Countries, is another case in point, showing the substantial funding city councils and national governments have to undertake to attract new investors. Taking into account the number of newly-created jobs and the kind of products involved, this seems a questionable policy.

FROM HOLLANDIA TO SUPERCONFEX: MACINTOSH AND THE RESTRUCTURING OF THE CLOTHING INDUSTRY

Once textile, clothing and footwear industry were essential to the employment in Nijmegen. The fact that the number of unskilled labourers was above average level and wages were relatively low had strongly encouraged industry to settle in the Nijmegen region (see chapter 2).

From the mid-1960s a sharp drop in employment was seen, which was due to a large-scale international restructuring. Increasing wage costs and an emerging labour shortage in the Netherlands were the reasons why industry transferred its manufacturing activities to the so-called "low-wage countries". The substantial flow of cheap commodities manufactured in these countries to the Netherlands caused a further drop in employment, because the smaller companies that had not changed over to internationalization proved to be unable to cope with this competition. Since the 1960s, 4,000 jobs in the manufacturing of textiles, clothing and footwear have been lost in the city of Nijmegen. Over the last few years the level of employment in those sectors has soared to a mere few hundred jobs. With the growth and restructuring of the MacIntosh organization as an example, we will examine the international developments in the clothing industry and its effects on employment in Nijmegen. Founded by the *Staatsmijnen Limburg* (the Limburg state mines) in the 1930s, MacIntosh (for over 50 percent owned by *DSM (Chemie)*, a state enterprise, grew into the largest clothing company in Western Europe after World War II. During the 1960s this expansion was accomplished especially by taking over existing Dutch companies that had well-known brands. In 1968, Nijmegen witnessed the take-over of "De Kievit" workshops employing approximately 250 people as well as that of "Bendien-Smits", with a labour force of 180 people two years later. "De Kievit" was left a basic production unit after the reorganization. The press-room, the cutting room and the sales department were scrapped. "Bendien-Smits" closed its Nijmegen plant.

In the 1970s, when the period of MacIntosh' expansion into Belgium and the Netherlands came to an end, international aetivities became increasingly important. These activities had already started long before when production was put out to East European workshops (late 1950s) and to South-east Asia (late 1960s). Servicing the latter region, a commercial business firm, Mac International, was set up which, operating from the Hong

Kong centre, co-ordinated the purchase of cheap and simple clothing from South Korea, Taiwan and the Philippines. Besides putting out production, the organization introduced new plants in Portugal, Brazil and Tunesia.

The MacKenzel company, set up in 1973, is one of the eighteen clothing companies in Tunesia, which were introduced by Dutch firms between 1973 and 1975. The firms have received support from the Dutch Government for transferring the manufacture to Tunesia. Moreover, the Dutch Government has given the guarantee to reimburse for all costs concerning damage incurred in Tunesia and has offered financial help for investments in this country.

Apart from the aforementioned reasons and its low-wage level, Tunesia had a special appeal to the Dutch clothing industry, for it offered a multitude of facilities. On top of tax exemptions in the Netherlands and the unhampered transfer of profits, the Tunesian Government guaranteed a peaceful working climate as well. Moreover, Tunesia has given foreign companies the guarantee that all losses owing to possible expropriation will be compensated for and that capital (i.e. machinery) can be freely transferred to the Netherlands in case of close-down of the Tunesian-based company.

Within the Tunesian economy the foreign companies are isolated manufacturing plants, which is due to the fact that only exports are allowed, a measure which protects the small indigenous companies.

Recent trends have shown that the emergence of foreign clothing companies does not give the least guarantee of a stable industrial development. According to MacIntosh, galloping inflation and the consequent rise in wage costs cause the manufacturing costs to be relatively high compared to other "low-wage countries". This accounts for the fact that in 1984 MacKenzel announced a reduction in labour force.

For the Netherlands the MacIntosh transfer has meanwhile been concluded. After the closure of "Hollandia Kievit" in 1981, its manufacturing in the Benelux, in 1971 still accounting for 9,000 jobs, had been reduced to a single company: "Bendien-Smits" in Almelo. Apart from that, two large clothing factories in Portugal and Tunesia remained. After this MacIntosh had its hands free to buy clothing anywhere in the world at the lowest prices possible and place orders for production with the location offering the most favourable conditions. If these conditions are subject to change, MacIntosh can promptly react to it. By 1984 MacIntosh gave the green light to another competition battle on the Dutch clothing market by introducing 20 large selling branches known as Superconfex. The organization's aim to expand its interests in trade and service, however, does not remain with the clothing branch. In this process the most speech-making event has been the take-over of the *Kwantum-hallen* organization early 1986. With *Superconfex* and *Kwantum-hallen* under its roof, MacIntosh has come back to Nijmegen again, however, as a retailer this time.

NIJMEGEN AND KAOHSIUNG: THANKS TO PHILIPS A LINK BETWEEN TWO CITIES?

The report on the division of labour between the Philips plants in Nijmegen and Kaohsiung (Taiwan) in this section of the chapter describes the internationalization of Philips' manufacturing in the electronics sector and its effects on employment.

In 1953 Philips Nijmegen was set up as an assembly plant with a labour force of 5 people. Except for a slight recession during the early 1980s, the employment offered at this plant has been on the increase, particularly so as a result of the development of the chip production, and amounted to approximately 3,000 people in 1986. Hence, Nijmegen locates one of the largest producers of semi-conductors in Europe and has the only Philips plant manufacturing ICs (Integrated Circuits) in the Netherlands.

Furthermore, the range of production includes diodes, transistors and lasers.

Forced by, amongst other things, international competition and in imitation of Japanese and US multinationals, Philips made the first move towards international restructuring of the semi-conductor industry, which was just getting off the ground at that time in 1967.

In Kaohsiung in Taiwan a plant was opened, the first European plant in this country. Besides considerations concerning competition, it was the facilities offered by the Taiwanese Government, which prompted settling in Taiwan, a low-wage country. These 'facilities' included, for instance, low taxes, free exportation of profits after taxation, infrastructural works provided for by Taiwan, free imports and exports of machinery and semi-products, long working hours, and the lack of independent labour unions. Employment in Taiwan experienced a substantial growth. In 1969 Philips Kaohsiung employed a mere 950 people, in 1986 this number had gone up to 7,300, in particular as a result of the expansion of the chip production.

The manufacturing process of ICs consists of four stages. In the first stage the monocrystalline silicon is prepared as the basic material for the chip. In the second stage, the diffusion stage, a semi-product is manufactured by applying the circuit diagrams onto the material. The third stage entails two steps. Firstly, the circuits are legged, whereafter they can be connected to other electronic systems ('bonding') and secondly, the chip is packaged ('packaging'). In the fourth and final stage the chip is measured and tested.

The first two stages, which are high grade in technological respect, and the most capital-intensive, are specifically taking place in the Nijmegen plant. Furthermore, the Nijmegen plant also specializes in Development & Research of ICs. Taiwan is charged with the assembly, which is the labour-intensive third stage and since 1974 it has also taken care of (a part of) the final testing.

Additionally, during the 1970s the restructuring and the internationalization of the manufacturing of chips fuelled the introduction of plants in South Korea (the entire assembly of the Metal Oxyd Semiconductor (MOS) chip has been transferred to this country), Hong Kong, the Philippines (assembly of diodes and transistors) and Brazil.

The division of labour between the Philips plants in Nijmegen and Kaohsiung as described above has still been carried on through to the present day, though the last few years have witnessed some changes, particularly so as a result of developments in automation. For example, thanks to the so-called Mega project, Nijmegen's position as a centre of Research & Development has grown stronger. The aim of this project, in which with Dutch and West German government support Philips and Siemens have joined hands, is to produce and develop the 'static chip' with a capacity of well over one million bits (the one-megabit chip). This calls for spectacular changes in the manufacturing process. In 1985 the building of FAB 87 was started, the first mass production of megachips is planned to take place there by the end of 1988.

In Taiwan Philips has not been idle either. No longer can the chip plant in Kaohsiung simply be looked upon as an inexpensive assembly and testing plant, for in the year 1987 the technological high-grade diffusion stage was taking place there as well.

These developments are closely related to efforts of the Taiwanese Government to motivate Philips to transfer its know-how by means of cooperative agreements. What's more, these developments are in line with the new Philips strategy concerning other product sectors to include a number of Third World countries into its worldwide manufacturing structure. This relates to changing conditions concerning location of the Philips production plants in a number of Third World countries. On the one hand, Philips Nijmegen, amongst others, has developed machinery which enables the assembly of ICs to be computerized. Consequently, the wage differences between Philips plants in Western Europe and Third World countries have less of an impact. On the other hand, some manufacturing plants in Third World countries have become more important for Philips owing to their locations, favourably close to or within markets which have strongly grown in significance and on which Philips is focusing its attention more and more. The Far East in particular, e.g. Japan, tends to become more important as an outlet for Philips, also with respect to IC semi-products. This is not only due to the rise in sales of electronics consumer goods within these countries, but chiefly to the fact that increasingly more manufacturers and (potential) buyers of Philips have become active in this part of the world.

ORGANIZATIONAL STRUCTURE AND LONG-TERM POLICIES OF A MULTINATIONAL: NUTRICIA

Nutricia is the leading company in the Netherlands in baby and infant food and in the coffee and chocolate sector. This section takes a closer look at the restructuring policies which the organization has carried out since the second half of the 1970s. Key concepts in this process were concentration, specialization and internationalization. In 1983 this company with a labour force of 2,261 people (of which 38 percent was employed abroad) reported a turnover of 574 million Dutch guilders and its nett profits were a good 22 million Dutch guilders. 85 Percent of this turnover was gained by selling within the EEC (including the Netherlands). Moreover, Nutricia exports its goods all over the world.

Nutricia Holland distinguishes three product groups. The first group is Nutricia (baby and infant food, and dietary and special products), the second is Nutremia (evaporated milk, chocolate, margarine and fats, fruit juices) and the last one

Luycks (mustard, vinegar, canned fruits, jams, snacks and mashed potato). For production in the Netherlands the Nutricia organization has six manufacturing companies, one of them is located in Cuijk a/d Maas. This company specializes in the manufacture of consumer goods and semi-products, such as the semi-products for baby and dietary foods.

Within Nutricia International the company's activities abroad are organized in four subsidiaries. This implies that Nutricia B.V. in Zoetermeer takes care of the exportation of goods manufactured in the Netherlands and Belgium, while Nutricia SA (Madrid) and Nutricia EpE (Athens) service the Spanish and the Greek markets, respectively. The manufacture for the latter two is mainly taking place in Belgium and Spain. Finally, Nibb-it International Ltd. in Great Britain is primarily engaged in the packaging and selling of salty Nibb-it biscuits. Another task of the Nutricia International subsidiary is internationalizing Nutricia e.g. by expanding its exports, entering into co-operations with other enterprises and embarking on manufacturing abroad.

Until the early 1970s Nutricia had known just one take-over, that is, that of Lacto, a dairy factory in Cuijk a/d Maas in 1924. With the take-over of 'N.V. Preservenbedrijf' (snacks and freeze-dried goods) in 1970, Nutricia made the first move towards *extension of the basis* (in order to consolidate existing market shares and to extend them, if possible) and *diversification* (spread of risk by specializing in a wider range of products). This was followed by the take-over of SVZ (canned food) and of Remia (oils, fats, and margarines) and Luycks B.V. (sauces, mustard and vinegar). Due to stagnations in the market, increasing competition and a rise in costs, this policy was hardly effective.

In 1977 Nutricia launched a restructuring operation, with the *concentration of activities* and *internationalization* as key concepts. Since then, the concentration of bottled liquid goods in Zoetermeer and powder products in Cuijk have come under the heading 'concentration of activities'. Ultimately, Remia, Luycks and SVZ were sold again in 1979, 1980 and 1982, respectively.

From 1976 'internationalization' has been realized by expanding the exports as well as enlarging the number of plants abroad. Particularly, in the child and dietary food sector attention was increasingly focused on the countries abroad. Cooperation with other companies active in the same sector was considered necessary, also because competition from, amongst others, Nestlé was breathing in the neck.

The first step of this 'growth through internationalization' was taken in 1981 when Nutricia merged with Cow & Gate, a British company exclusively manufacturing child food. This company, member of the Unigate organization, accounted in 1981 for 40 percent of the British baby and child food market and was exporting to the ex-colonies of the United Kingdom on a large scale.

The merge was in line with Nutricia's aim to internationalize and specialize. This considerably strengthened Nutricia's position internationally, for it implied that the company had conquered a major share in the baby and infant food markets in Britain, South Asia and parts of Africa, while Nutricia itself had always been strongly represented on the Dutch, West European and Indonesian markets. Moreover, a consequence of the merge was that the research efforts put less of a pressure on the turnover and that the company attained an increasing flexibility owing to the acquisition of a second manufacturing company (operating in the baby, infant and child food sector), in addition to the plant in Cuijk.

HYSTER: THE POWER OF A MULTINATIONAL ENTERPRISE

Hyster is one of the various multinational enterprises which set up business in Nijmegen and environs during the postwar period. The theme of this section is the developments in this enterprise in the early 1980s. The worldwide reorganization carried through by the Hyster organization in this period gives an idea of the range of possibilities open to multinationals to *transfer production and employment on an international level.*

Hyster Nijmegen is a subsidiary of *Hyster Company*, based in Portland in Oregon, USA. The Nijmegen plant, set up in 1952, was the first manufacturing company of Hyster in Europe. Hyster started here with a labour force of 25 people, a number which rose to nearly 700 by the end of the 1970s and successively went down again to approximately 380 in 1985.

Hyster Nijmegen is made up of two parts: a central depot for spare parts and a plant manufacturing fork lift trucks. Local manufacture involves the assembly of fork lift trucks developed in Portland, USA, with the production of eight different models as a result. Nijmegen neither has a Development Department, nor does production planning and marketing take place here. It is the European head office in Basingstoke, Great Britain, which is responsible for these activities. This procedure shows that Hyster Company has an extremely tight, centralized organizational structure. The management of the Nijmegen plant cannot exert its influence on the development of production planning in Basingstoke. In 1983 the then Managing Director hinted that the only thing he had to do was to manufacture the goods that were to be sold at the lowest costs possible.

During the 1978-1982 period, just before the major reorganization in 1983, the Nijmegen Hyster plant made a nett profit of about 55 million Dutch guilders. A sum of at least 18 million guilders of this profit was transferred to the parent company in the form of dividends. Moreover, during this five-year period another 47 million guilders were paid to Hyster Portland in the form of licence rights. In 1982 a huge recession in turnover and returns was reported. Still, the Nijmegen plant achieved a five-million-guilder nett profit in this year.

Of old Hyster was a familiar name for many Nijmegen inhabitants. After all, year after year the company had been making a profit, the Americans paid their employees just a little more than the majority of the employers in the region and their policies concerning social provisions were reasonable. Yet, they were not on such a good footing with the labour unions. Intimidation and putting a tail on union members at work marked the hostile attitude. The works council was composed in such a way that the workers on the shop-floor, and therefore members of the FNV (labour union) within the enterprise were underrepresented to a significant extent. What's more, the works council and the labour unions had been badly informed about the running of the company.

What is true for many multinational corporations also holds for Hyster: the returns of the entire organization as a whole are key priority. Decisions about, for instance, the composition of the production range of Hyster Nijmegen have to be consistent with the strategy of the entire organization. The lingering economic crisis and the worldwide decreasing demand for fork lift trucks were the trigger for Hyster Company to secretly examine the possibilities to cut back on costs. Employers, local Managing Directors and even members of the company's Board of Commissioners were ignorant of the decisions taken until they leaked out into the press. An implication of the principle that manufacturing had to take place at the location with the lowest production costs was that each individual Hyster plant was being compared with potential locations elsewhere in the world. For Hyster plants in Belgium and the Netherlands and in some American states the outcome of this comparison turned out to be negative. The reorganization round started in the home country, the USA, were the various states accommodating Hyster plants were played off against each other. Requests to governments for financial support were invariably accompanied by threats of closure if no (sufficient) help was forthcoming. One of the states which lost the 'battle' for the highest bid was Oregon, whose offer of financial support was several million dollars less than that of Illinois.

Hence, the manufacturing plant in Portland, Oregon, where once the foundation for the Hyster organization had been laid, was closed down, and the activities in Illinois extended. Next, Europe got in focus.

New developments took place in Ireland, a tax heaven where even previously two modern plants had been introduced, followed by one more in Irvine, Scotland. The highest bidder, the Thatcher Government in Great Britain, was rewarded with the promise that the Hyster plant in Irvine was to grow into a plant with a labour force of 1,000 employees. In exchange, Hyster received financial help amounting to 40 million guilders for the investments promised, and another 42 million guilders for retraining. Together these sums amounted to almost 50 percent of the total investment. Furthermore, the employees in Scotland were pressurized in such a way that they accepted a 15-percent pay reduction in exchange for keeping their jobs in an area that was severely hit by unemployment.

On Nijmegen these developments had a negative effect. Owing to the joint efforts of labour unions and employees the plan to progressively reduce the manufacture in Nijmegen to nil could be checked, chiefly because Hyster had not taken the slightest notice of a number of legislative measures, but still another 165 people were made redundant. Yet, a judgment prevented Hyster from transferring parts of the manufacture to other Hyster plants before January 1, 1988.

The international reorganization carried through by the Hyster organization in the early 1980s shows that the power of multinational corporations is not confined to finding the most favourable and cheapest locations for manufacture in the world, they can also stipulate for locations offered on the most favourable terms by playing off governments and employees against each other on an international level. In other words, Hyster was not only looking for the best locations, but they created these themselves. This influence is apparent in stipulations for various subsidies and other government incentives, and in the heavy toll on pay exacted from employees by putting them under pressure. The extra opportunities made available by restructuring internationally might be a reason in itself to start restructuring internationally. In this case it gave Hyster the opportunity to have governments and employees pay even more for the presence of "the Company" in a specific region or country.

BRISTOL MYERS: AN INCENTIVE OF HALF A MILLION GUILDERS PER JOB

After ample discussion in 1982 the Nijmegen city council gave the green light to the arrival of *Bristol Myers Company* (BMC), an American organization, in Nijmegen. This part deals with the *determining factors* for BMC to choose Nijmegen as their *location.* We will further consider the problems related to the use of breast-feeding substitutes in Third World countries e.g. those produced by Bristol Myers.

With a turnover of 3,5 thousand million guilders, plants in more than 80 countries and 35,000 people employed all over the world, BMC is one of the most prominent multinationals in the world. BMC started off as a pharmaceutic enterprise. The manufacturing of pharmaceutic and medical goods is still the essential activity of the company, In addition there are three other main groups falling under BMC: consumer goods, health care and food products. The latter group is known as Mead Johnson.

In Nijmegen, Mead Johnson is specifically manufacturing breast-feeding substitutes for babies and dietary food for adults. Production, which started by the end of 1984, is mainly aimed at export outside the EEC and Europe, while raw materials (e.g. milk, soya and the like) are being bought in the Netherlands. Thus, each day 50,000 litres of milk from the region are delivered at the company's door. The mayor and aldermen are expecting the company to provide 125 jobs eventually.

BMC's preference for Nijmegen as the place of business for the organization's first activity in the dairy sector within the EEC can be traced back to three factors. One of them was the presence of many well-skilled labourers with experience in the dairy sector. Furthermore, Coberco, a dairy company in Arnhem, had to contend with an overcapacity of labour.

The second factor was the EEC incentives for export. Since the EEC has been wrestling with problems of large dairy surpluses for a long time, attempts have been made to stimulate exports to non-EEC countries by offering so-called export restitutions. These restitutions imply that exporters and manufacturers exporting dairy products at prices below the guaranteed price holding within the EEC are being paid the difference from public funds. BMC enjoys the lasting benefit of this restitution policy. (Apart from these export incentives, the EEC tries to get rid of a part of her dairy surpluses by processing it into feed and by giving food aid).

The last factor determining the location of the company in Nijmegen, a region burdened by a high unemployment rate, was the facilities offered by the Dutch state and the city of Nijmegen. For instance, the WIR and IPR incentives offered by the state meant that some ten million guilders were put at BMC's disposal as investment support. The city of Nijmegen sold more building land to BMC than was considered necessary according to the existing standards and this at a lower than usual price, which, in the end, boiled down to the fact that the company had been subsidized for a sum of Dfl. 110,000.-. Moreover, as a consequence of the size of the building site requested by BMC, a road had to be moved. The costs of this project were also at the city's expenses (Dfl. 305,000,-). Finally, the city granted BMC a special exemption from the Nuisance Act, which enabled this company to build high powder silos.

The emergence of Bristol Myers in Nijmegen has raised many questions with a number of council members but also with a large number of people and groupings outside the city council. These questions concern the use of BMC baby food in Third World countries.

Over the last few years breast-feeding substitutes manufactured by industry have won ground at a very high rate from breast-feeding itself in various Third World countries. Yet, the necessary conditions for a safe use of artificial baby food such as clean water, good hygiene and a sufficient income are not met in many developing countries. On top of that, evidence from research has repeatedly proved the merits of breast-feeding in comparison with bottle-feeding and revealed that in the Third World bottle-feeding brings about a rise in the death and disease rates.

In May 1981 these considerations led the WHO (the World Health Organization of the United Nations) to accept an "International Code of Conduct for putting breast-feeding substitutes on the market". The aim of this "code of conduct" is to restrict the advertising and selling of artificial baby food. However, the code is badly complied with as it is no more than a recommendation.

Besides companies such as Nutricia, Nestlé and the Coöperatieve Condensfabriek Friesland, it appears that so far Bristol Myers has also failed to observe the WHO code when selling baby food. It is clear that BMC does not think the code acceptable and considers it an arbitrary attempt to put a ban on lawful trade in the name of health.

During the council debate on the planned establishment of BMC in Nijmegen a minority in the city council asked the mayor and aldermen to put forward a request to BMC to observe the WHO code. Yet, against his better judgment, the mayor claimed that the company was already observing the code and that, for countries where the code is not yet applicable, BMC had its own code. A comparison between the WHO and the BMC codes revealed that the latter is vague and far from being complete. By devious means the BMC code gives the impression that it is not a serious matter if certain rules and legislations are not being observed. A more general comment needs to be added to the criticism expressed above.

Subsidized dumping of dairy surpluses on Third World markets often has a negative effect on the home production of milk in developing countries, for buying milk from abroad tends to be cheaper than setting up a dairy industry at home. An increase in unemployment, which is already high, and consolidation of international relations of dependence will be the consequences of this policy.

The effects of the BMC settlement on employment in Nijmegen are questionable, for jobs will probably be lost at other dairy companies whereas BMC has been given an occasional subsidy of about half a million guilders per job. Meanwhile they get permanent help _ from public funds _ for export under the EEC policies concerning agriculture.

Chapter 4

DUTCH FIRMS IN DEVELOPING COUNTRIFS FOR INSTANCE, INDIA

Fons van der Velden

The role of foreign companies in the process of industrialisation in Third World countries has generally been assessed positively by the present Indian and Dutch Governments. For example, the former Dutch Secretary of State _ Mr. Bolkestein _ declared that, amongst others, in the Netherlands "*The key role of economic activity in the development of the Third World has been neglected too long*". According to him, "*underdevelopment is mainly due to lack of rain, political instability and inefficient administration*", and, in his point of view, "*multinational corporations _ regardless of exceptions _ have a favourable effect on the development of the Third World. The capital flow, the technical flow, management techniques and the labour relations, too: in all these fields Dutch companies can do a lot in the Third World and thcy may also set an example*".

Yet, more and more serious questions have been raised concerning the growing influence and the increasing power of multinational corporations both in the West and in the Third World. Several studies point to the negative effects and potential dangers of foreign investments on the developmental process of Third World countries. These studies do not only considcr thc *political influcncc* of foreign companies but they also come to the conclusion that international firms in the Third World are often *producing goods which contribute little if anything to the construction of the country.* To illustrate this, Dutch companies in India are manufacturing clock radios, hifi equipment, shampoos, hormone preparations, tonics, cosmetics, tapes and talcum powders. As a rule, the products launched by the West are meant for a small number of people at the top and they are produced according to their tastes. Within the scope of this chapter it is impossible to discuss all the political, social, cultural, economic and other effects of foreign investments in the Third World. The discussion in the next sections is based on a study which was carried out recently by a research team from Jawaharlal Nehru University of New Delhi and from the Third World Centre of Nijmegen University (The Netherlands) and it will deal with some of the effects, primarily economic, of foreign investments in India.

INDIA INCREASINGLY IN FOCUS

The following examples are certainly not representative of all countries of "the Third World", for in many respects India is a relatively strong developing country. Measured by the size of the value added, it ranks fourteenth among the world's industrial nations (1983). This gigantic subcontinent is richly endowed with minerals and raw materials; its public sector is relatively large. Despite great poverty and huge income differences, the home market with about 750 million inhabitants is extremely large. It has many well-qualified executive workers (technicians, doctors etc.) and besides a sizeable small-scale industry there are many big domestic manufacturing enterprises as well. Nevertheless, these examples do illustrate the effect of private foreign investments in a developing country; in many Third World countries that are not so strong in economic respect, consequences are likely to be more dramatic.

In recent years Dutch companies have considerably expanded their activities. The Dutch ministry of Development Cooperation played and is still playing an active and supportive part in it. This is, amongst others, demonstrated by several initiatives which have been taken since 1981. Early 1981, Mr De

Koning, M.A., the then minister of Development Cooperation, sent a heavy delegation (including Claus, The Dutch prince consort) to India "*to investigate to which extent relations between India and the Netherlands can be broadened in the fields of trade, economy, finances, methods of agriculture, science and culture*". In the memorandum signed at the end of the visit, it was pleaded that the commercial relations should be expanded and the activities of private trade and industry and those of the ministry should be more closely interlocked. The Indo-Dutch Business Council, founded in 1982, is also supporting this line of policy. In 1981, a Rotterdam delegation visited India to study, amongst other things, the possibilities for Dutch participation in improving Bombay port. Early 1983, Mr Bolkestein M.A., LL.M., the then Secretary of State of Foreign Trade went to India to negotiate about "*the necessary expansion of economic interrelations*", which resulted in an economic agreement. In "*Reverification of Bilateral Development Cooperation*" and "*Development Cooperation and Employment*", the green papers published at that time by Mrs Schoo, M.A., the then minister of Development Cooperation and at present the Dutch Ambassador in New Delhi, a further privatization of Dutch Development Cooperation was pleaded for. The Royal Family keep supporting this approach. Early 1986, Beatrix, the Dutch Queen and Claus, the prince consort, went to India with 22 entrepreneurs following in their track. During the trip, Mr Van Den Broek, Secretary of State for Foreign Affairs declared: "*Though this state visit is not primarily meant to sell Holland, that is, Dutch enterprises, we can still talk of a satisfying combination*". Recently, March 1987, he and Mr Lubbers, the Dutch Prime minister, went on a visit to India again. A cooperative agreement to improve the dredging infrastructure in India was signed. Dutch contribution: almost 625 crore rupees.

POLITICAL AND ECONOMIC DEVELOPMENTS IN INDIA

The aforementioned activities of Dutch entrepreneurs and Dutch Government were closely linked up with economic developments in India itself. Since its Independence, the attitude of Indian Government towards foreign investing has changed quite often. From early 1980 onwards when Indira Gandhi and her Congress Party were re-elected, it has become evident that the restrictions concerning the growth of foreign enterprises have clearly been eased and that sectors that were previously under Indian government control have been thrown open to foreign investors. The control of Indian monopoly houses (such as Tata and Birla) as well as foreign enterprises has relaxed. *Liberalization, pragmatism, efficiency and export export-led growth* have become the key concepts in formulating the policy. After Indira Gandhi died (end 1984) her successor, her son Rajiv, has been rigorously pursuing this policy. Immediately after he was appointed Prime Minister, in an interview with *Time*, an American weekly, he stated that India would throw open her economy to foreign investors and imported technology from abroad even more. "*Now the position of our economy has been reinforced so much that we need new injections. And, therefore we are welcoming multinational corporations*". In economic respect, this policy is linked up with the fact that, in 1981, India, prompted by a serious crisis in the balance of payments, negotiated a 5 thousand million dollar loan (US dollars) from IMF. Just as in other countries which had previously been granted a loan such as Jamaica, Peru and Tanzania, this has led to a structural adjustment of socio-economic policies to IMF demands. The key elements of this adjustment are, for instance, a wider margin for domestic and foreign private enterprises, greater dependency on foreign technology, markets and finances, pay freeze and cutbacks on the public services, minimal as they are, and on public allowances in general.

WHY INDIA?

One wonders why it is appealing to Dutch companies to expand their businesses in India. A complex of factors is involved here. Firstly, despite the fact that approximately more than half the population lives below the poverty line, India has an enormous domestic *market*. Secondly, the *wages* are invitingly low.

The wages of unskilled labourers in the electrotechnical branch, for example, are on average about 650 rupees a month. Thirdly, Indian Government has provided an adequate *infrastructure* in the form of roads, ports and communications facilities. Furthermore, it gives foreign investors full freedom *to transfer profits, dividends* and *royalties* abroad. In addition, the authoritarian-repressive rule of the Congress Party prevents industrial unrest. Finally, their activities in India allow foreign companies to set up *joint ventures* in other developing countries in collaboration with Indian companies. Thus, the cheap labour of the Indian worker can also be deployed abroad.

DUTCH COMPANIES IN INDIA

What are the effects of the presence of Dutch companies in India on Indian economy? Before giving a reply a brief survey will be presented of the nature and the size of foreign investments in India's economy in general and of Dutch ones in particular.

From way back British private investments took a key position in Indian economy. However, since India became independent, the interests of investments from the United States, West Germany, Japan, Italy, Switzerland and France have substantially grown. In qualitative respect as well, important developments have taken place. In the first place, today foreign investors are especially interested in the most dynamic, technologically advanced sectors of Indian economy. Secondly, activities of foreign companies are increasingly more realized in collaboration with private or state-owned Indian companies. Thirdly, now more than in the colonial time, foreign companies are interested in the Indian market. The form of foreign influence is subject to change. Dutch investing in India can be subdivided into: 1. subsidiaries entirely owned by the parent company (ABN Bank and AMRO Bank), 2. subsidiaries with majority participation from the Netherlands (such as *Hindustan Lever*, a Unilever subsidiary), 3. subsidiaries with minority participation, the so-called FERA companies (such as Organon and Philips) and 4.

companies which have a licence agreement with a Dutch company or which cooperate with them on a purely technical basis (such as Stanicarbon, DSM). As regards this subdivision it should be noted that in case of minority participations and technical collaborations, the actual control of the company in India still remains with the parent company in the Netherlands.

As far as the spread over various sectors of the economy is concerned, a few data will be given. About two third of all foreign investing has taken place in manufacture, 14 percent in the extraction of oil, and about 12 percent in plantations. Within industry, foreign capital is concentrated in machine and chemical industries. Nowhere else is the dominance of foreign companies so strong as in the drug and pharmaceutical industries, in which 66 multinational corporations control 80 percent of total manufacture, and annually they transfer 50 percent of the starting investments to the home country. The manufacture of, for instance, cigarettes, detergents, typewriters, electrodes, fertilizers, glycerin, explosives, batteries (*Union Carbide*) and lamps is almost entirely dominated by foreign companies.

Nowadays total *Dutch* private investments in India amount to approximately 40 crores. This is only 6 percent of total foreign investments in India and it pales into insignificance when compared to the size of the investments from Great Britain (61 percent of the total) and the United States (21 percent). Nevertheless, in some sectors of Indian economy Dutch influence is of decisive importance. For instance, *Hindustan Lever*, the Unilever subsidiary controls the detergent sector and the company figures largely in the foodstuffs industry in general. Having taken over Brooke Bond (in 1984), Unilever controls 95 percent of the tea market in India and Pakistan. Hindustan Lever is among India's largest companies. It ranks fifth in various lists of the ten companies at the top (concerning assets), second (concerning turnover) and even first (concerning profits). *Philips*, called PEICO in India, employs approximately about 7,000 people. ranks 35th on the list of the largest enterprises in India and i production range extends itself from batteries, radios, TV sets to medical and telecommunication equipment. What's more, the company dominates almost the entire light bulb industry by means of *Hind Lamps* and *ELMI*, the Indian subsidiaries. The same holds true for the radio market.

Since (Burmah) Shell was nationalized in 1976, the *Royal Shell Group* has always been present in India through a participation in *National Organic Chemical Industries India Ltd (NOCIL)*, a mushrooming petrochemical industry, and in *Wavin India Ltd.* The latter is among the largest producers of PVC pipes (for irrigation and drinking-water supply) in India. *AKZO* is present in India through a technical cooperation and an equity share participation of *Century Enka* (predominantly synthetic yarns) and *Organon*, a pharmaceutical company. *VMF-Stork* participates in India in *Storec Screens India* and *Stormac India*, two relatively new companies. Some 450 smaller Dutch companies own a subsidiary in India or have a technical, or other form of, collaboration with an Indian enterprise.

CAPITAL EXPORTS

Will Dutch investors be able *to live up to this idea* of giving a positive contribution to India, as former Dutch secretary of State, Mr Bolkestein called it? In the field of *capital supplies* they certainly won't. Compared to Indian home industry and parent companies, foreign companies are making large profits. According to government figures in India, on average these are about 170 to 300 percent higher than those of domestic companies. For some companies in India, these high profits enable them to earn enough to repay starting investments in one or two years. Dutch companies, too, are making relatively high profits in India. The gross profit of Hindustan Lever, for instance, has risen from 60 percent of the total equity share capital in 1980 to 140 percent in 1981. On an international level the profits are high, which is evident from the fact that in 1981 Unilever employed a mere 3 percent of its labour force in India whereas 18 percent of its profits were realized there. The outcome of these high profits is a vigorous growth of the companies. Between 1973 and 1981 the capital growth rate of Hindustan Lever, Century Enka and PEICO was 653, 400 and 297 percent respectively. High profits did not only result in rapid growth, but also in voluminous transfers of capital to foreign countries, which contributed to a deficit in the balance of payments. According to estimates quoted in the *Economic Times* (Bombay), a total of Rs 516 crores containing dividends, royalties, technical assistence and interest was tranferred to foreign countries in the 1965-1978 period. The annual increase was approximately 11 percent, about 4 percent above the inflation rate. Other estimates are pointing in the same direction. A survey of Rajiv Sau, an economist, says that in the 1970s during seven years the capital exports by foreign companies exceeded their capital imports by Rs 210 crores a year. In the 1975-1980 period all Dutch companies in India together transferred more capital to the Netherlands in the form of dividends etc., than they brought into India.

If we implicate exports and imports (of raw materials, components and capital goods) into the estimates, the picture becomes more differentiated at first. Between 1974 and 1978 it was during two years only that the capital flow from India was more substantial than the capital brought into India by Dutch companies. However, this picture is primarily biased due to exports by Hindustan Lever, mostly containing goods produced by third parties. Leaving Hindustan Lever aside, a deficit of Rs 28 crores emerges, the actual capital export is likely to be a greater still, because of internal transfers between subsidiaries, a fact which can hardly be verified by people from outside the company. Overcharging and undercharging on imports and exports allows the parent company to let the profits pop up at the place where it is most lucrative for the enterprise. With respect to some sectors, the volume of the capital flow leaving India is much larger than that of the transfers which are immediately visible. This is due to this *transfer pricing* system. As it appears from confidential papers by Indian Government a number of

Dutch companies in India are making use of this system as well. Regarding Philips, for example, it came to light that at one time the company exported light bulbs for a price lower than the production cost. (The bulbs had been exported to Holland for half a rupee and they were sold for 5 rupees a piece. Only the labels had been changed). Studies referring to other companies reveal that this system of transfer pricing has caused the export of large sums of money from India. As far as the pharmaceutical industry in India is concerned, it has been calculated that the invisible capital export is about one and a half times as big as the visible, registered capital export.

TRANSFER OF TECHNOLOGY

Besides the capital flow, Mr Bolkestein, the former Dutch Secretary of State, presented, amongst others, *technical assistence* as an important legitimization of Dutch involvement in India. In connection with Dutch companies in India, it appears that it happens quite often that the transfer of technology does not live up to the expectations. Usually, technology is *sold* instead of being actually passed on. This transfer of technology is in most cases limited to one company and the use of it is subject to restrictions. Know-how should not be passed on to other companies and cannot be used to produce for export purposes. Moreover, imported technology, which Rajiv Gandhi wants to expand, often leads to compulsory imports of raw materials and components by the Indian subsidiary. Another common problem is that the imported technology has regularly gone out of date or that it is not adjusted to the pattern of demand in India. Few companies in India are undertaking *Research & Development* activities, in fact, of the Dutch companies Unilever and Philips are the sole ones which do. It happens quite often that no actual research is being carried out, but a mere quality test instead.

However, this does not hold good for Unilever in India. The company has a central laboratory in Bombay, at which cheap Indian research labour is combined with high-quality (imported) equipment. On the one hand, research is focused on finding indigenous substitutes for imported products of which import has been, and still is, subject to restrictions imposed by Indian Government (such as edible oils and fats for soap); on the other hand _ as it appears _ matters are being studied which bear no relation to the production in India, but rather to that of the company at large.

EFFECTS WITH REGARD TO EMPLOYMENT

It is rather hard to estimate the *employment effect* of the presence of Dutch multinational corporations in India in a quantitative sense. It should be taken for granted that in a still primarily *peasant society* such as India, employment in industry is very limited as it is. Multinational corporations account for one percent of total employment and 13 percent of jobs in the manufacturing sector of the country. For each product and sector, however, huge differences can be observed, varying from 100 percent concerning starting motors and conductors to 9 percent in the cement industry. At the plants, Dutch companies employ a total of 25,000 labourers. Yet, this figure should not be considered to be the nett employment created, because the relation with indigenous industry should be taken into account as well. It happens quite often that large profits and rapid growth of foreign companies ruin the domestic producers operating in the same sector. This can be explained by the fact that, compared to indigenous small-scale units, multinational corporations have larger financing resources available; they are more able to organize the production process efficiently; they use modern marketing methods and they usually dispose of a well-functioning distribution network of their own. What's more, in many countries in the Third World consumers _ partly due to these factors _ tend to prefer products of foreign companies.

Owing to the concentration of the production in foreign hands, it regularly occurs that *employment* at indigenous units is *lost*. These tendencies are also noticeable in India. A familiar example is WIMCO, the Swedish match factory, which, through the years, has pushed a lot of small-sized match producers "off the market". This resulted in a nett loss of jobs in this sector. Similar problems are at issue with respect to some Dutch companies in India. The lamp sector is a good example. PEICO, and ELMI and Hind Lamps, its subsidiaries, dominate about 40 percent of the market. Yet they regulate the supply of crucial components, hence, the majority of the other lamp manufacturers in India directly depends on PEICO. In this way they are in control of almost the entire lamp industry in India. The outcome of this control and concentration is clear. In the early 1970s, there were 127 small-scale producers of light bulbs, in 1977 a mere 50 were left. It is not only in lamps that Philips has become so powerful in India, for plenty of other examples could be given. Though the detergent sector has been reserved for the small-scale sector, Hindustan Lever has retained its monopoly position here, so the number of jobs has fallen. Apparently, the tentative conclusion seems to be justified that the employment effect of a lot of foreign investments _ producing in a capital-intensive way instead of in a labour-intensive one _ is only small or even negative.

WAGES

The monthly *wages* earned by employees of Dutch companies in India vary from 400 to 1,700 rupees. Leaving negative exceptions aside, just as in most other foreign companies, they are 10 to 25 percent higher than those earned at indigenous companies of the same size operating in the same sector and the same region. This also holds true for the bulk of other foreign businesses. However, one comment should be added to this information at once: the real income of factory labourers in India is falling and at the moment it is as low as in 1960 or even in 1939. The wages earned at multinational corporations are above the average level, yet they are no exception to this general trend. Moreover, it turns out that the rise in pay of employees of Dutch companies in India is lagging behind the rise in turnover, in the gross profits and the value added. Furthermore, with respect to labour conditions and labour relations it is relevant that some Dutch companies in India are employing *daily labourers* and *temporary workers* to an increasing extent. They are not as expensive as workers on a permanent job, for labour legislation (progressive in itself) does not apply to them. At Hindustan Lever in Bombay, out of a total of 4,000 labourers 1,000 are holding temporary appointments or are working on daily wages.

INCREASING "SUBCONTRACTING"

Dutch companies in India, and Philips, Shell and Unilever in particular, are putting out more and more work to small-scale companies (*subcontracting*) (see chapter 1 as well). Subcontracting may occur in different forms depending on the nature of the production technology applied.

Affected by two factors, subcontracting has boomed since the early 1960s. Firstly, government policies played a decisive role. Several measures were taken to stimulate subcontracting and the growth of small-scale industry. They included "positive" measures (such as tax advantages, subsidies and credit facilities) and protective measures (such as the *Monopolies and Restrictive Trade Practices (MRTP) Act* and the *Foreign Exchange Regulation Act (FERA)*. Secondly, the recession of the mid-1960s played a major part. In the attempt to reduce costs and thus to stimulate earning capacity and growth, work was sub-contracted to small-scale companies in various sectors more regularly. Concerning the latter, a combination of factors comes in. In the first place, *production costs* in small-scale companies are usually *lower* than those of big businesses. Characteristic features of the small-scale sector are the absence of proper labour legislation, (the *Factories Act* solely applies to companies employing over 50 people), and a restricted collective bargaining power of labourers, which is due to the fact that labour relations still tend to be feudal. In an economy with a labour surplus, as is the case in India, this results in the wages paid at small-scale units being twice as low as those paid at big companies. Another major factor is that subcontracting gives big enterprises more scope *to react to changes in the market.* During a sales depression, employees at small-scale companies can be made redundant with more ease; the customer may delay the payment of bills, refuse to accept the goods, postpone quality testing etc. Because power is distributed unevenly, big companies frequently find it easy to pass on the problems to the small supplying companies. In this connection, it is interesting to note that studies have shown that in practice small-scale suppliers in India have granted relatively long-term commercial credits to big companies. Furthermore, subcontracting is increasingly used by managements of big (foreign) companies *to restrict the bargaining power of labour unions.* A small-scale company employs a limited number of people and, generally, the labour relations tend to be more personal in nature; therefore, less employees are organized and less industrial conflicts occur. This leads, just as the spread of activities over a large number of small companies, to less-interrupted supplies.

SUBCONTRACTING BY DUTCH COMPANIES

As already stated above, Dutch companies in India are putting out more and more work. Some examples: In 1979, labourers at the *Lipton Tea* plant in Calcutta (owned by Unilever's *Hindustan Lever*) went on strike demanding improvements in the labour situation and wages. The strike lasted approximately six months and the company was upset in such a way that it lost part of the tea market in India. To prevent such problems from occurring in future, immediately when the strike was over, the company's management set up a kind of assembly subcontracting: the packing of tea was distributed over some small-scale companies in the cities of Hyderabad, Nellore and Poona. Lipton Tea management said that production costs in these units (the extra transport costs included) were only as little as 40 percent of those in the Calcutta plant. Moreover, there is hardly any difference in labour productivity. Meanwhile, a large number of employees at the Calcutta plant was made redundant.

Wavin India Ltd., the Shell subsidiary, has put out the manufacture of small-diameter PVC pipes to four small-scale units. These four units, legally owned by others, are *de facto* controlled by Wavin, because they have been set up by Wavin, which is their sole customer. Wavin is the single supplier and buyer and it supplies the means of production, technical know-how, management and other forms of backing. Thus, Wavin can by-pass Indian legislation prescribing that the right to produce small-diameter PVC pipes is reserved for small-scale companies.

Since set-up, *Vicon India Ltd.* (subsidiary of Vicon, a Dutch company producing agricultural machinery) has been using subcontracting. Problems with the labour union caused the company to close down its plant in the city of Bangalore in 1984. Today all Vicon's products are manufactured by small-scale industry. Just like most companies, *PEICO (Philips India)* has put out the bulk of activities bearing no direct relation to the manufacturing process (such as cleaning, garden maintenance, security, transport etc.). But it is also using various other forms of subcontracting on a large scale. In recent years product subcontracting in particular has boomed. Nowadays among others "Philips" radios, black-and-white TV sets, mono casette players and batteries are all being made in small-scale companies. Labour union leaders working at Philips India say that today 60 percent of the company's total turnover is manufactured in the small-scale sector. It is a familiar fact that of late *Hindustan Lever* (Unilever) has transferred, amongst others, the production of *Sunlight* soap from the Bombay plant to three small-scale enterprises in the cities of Bangalore, Aurangabad and Poona. It is obvious that the key motives for it were cost considerations and undermining the negotiating power of the organized labourers in Bombay.

IS SMALL BEAUTIFUL?

In various scientific studies the effects of subcontracting are quite often assessed positively. As pros for big companies, reduction in costs and controlled supplies of components or products are mentioned. As pros for small-scale industry, they mention an increase in employment, transfer of technology and, sometimes, of capital, a guaranteed supply of raw materials and marketing of the manufacture. A great many Indian researchers do not agree. Nirmala Banarjee points out that usually no more jobs are created at the transfer of work from big to small-scale companies. The pay is generally too low to keep body and soul together; labour situations for the labourers _ primarily women and children _ are generally pathetic and the relation between employer and employee is often of a feudal nature. Moreover, reductions in costs are not passed on to the consumer and, from a macroeconomic point of view, growing product subcontracting leads to the worsening of income distribution. Another negative effect of this development is that, as stated before, the bargaining power of the organized labour movement gets affected by (the threat of) the transfer of labour. In most enterprises, especially at Philips and Unilever, quite a few industrial disputes are taking place continually, in which, apart from economic, often non-economic demands are at stake, such as the right to form free labour unions. Besides, in many companies active union members, for instance, those working at the Philips plant in the city of Poona, are victimised by the company's management. In those cases "*small*" is anything but "*beautiful*", as Schumacher, the famous economist, would have us believe.

CODE OF CONDUCT FOR MULTINATIONALS?

In India and various other Third World countries leftist politicians, scholars, labour unions and church-related groups have made many serious comments on the functioning of multinational corporations in developing countries. Years ago, Professor S.K. Goyal, an expert on foreign investments, once said about multinationals:

"*It is unfortunate that while we in India are quite sensitive to anything concerning our national honour and political independence, yet we do very little to meet challenges from within and the fast growing sector of the economy which shall never identify itself with India's national economic interest*".

It is striking that in general, little is expected from the UN code of conduct for *multinational corporations*. In a recent paper of the Non-Aligned Movement this is commented on as follows:

"..... *even the most perfect code could never force transnationals to channel their direct investments towards those branches that contribute to the economic progress of the underdeveloped countries unless they were highly profitable branches*".

In this connection Dan Gallan, General Secretary of the International Union of Food and Allied Workers (IUF) said that international codes are no more than a "*codification of the existing power relations between labour and capital*". As a reaction to the recent political failure to make multinational corporations toe the line, more and more initiatives have been taken from below in the West as well as in the Third World, to strengthen the democratic control of firms operating internationally. Outside the labour unions sectorial organisations such as *Foundation for Research in the Electrical Branch* (SOBE, predominantly Philips-oriented) and research institutions such as *SOMO (Foundation for Research on Multinational Corporations)* have emerged, supporting consumers and labour unionists to be a stronger opposing power to big companies. Moreover, the international labour movement still plays a crucial role.

Furthermore, development education has made people more aware of the outrageous practices of multinational corporations in the West as well as in the Third World. This has resulted in, amongst others, the organization of strong consumer campaigns, such as boycotts. Thus, of late, the Nestlé corporation in the United States was forced by a well-organized and efficiently held boycott campaign of the *International Nestlé Boycot Committee* to observe the regulations as laid down in the WHO Code regarding the sales of breast-milk substitutes.

Selected bibliography

N. Banerjee, Is small beautiful?, A.K. Bagchi & N. Banerjee (eds.), *Change and choice in Indian Industry*, Calcutta (K.P. Bagchi), 1981, pp. 279-295.

S. Baru, Self-reliance to dependence in Indian economic development, *Social Scientist*, nov. 1983, pp. 34-47.

F. Castro, *The world economic and social crisis; its somber prospects and the need to struggle if we are to survive*, New Delhi (PPH), 1983.

C.P. Chandrasekhar & P. Purkayastha, Transfer pricing in Indian drug industry; An estimate and implications, *Social Scientist*, jan. 1982, pp. 3-11.

U. Dhar, *The effects of multinational enterprises on employment in India*, Geneva (ILO), 1979.

S.K. Goyal, MNC's and Indian Economic Development, *Link* (Independence Day number), aug., 1980.

S.K. Goyal, K.S. Chalapati Rao, N. Kumar, *Small scale sector and big business*, New Delhi (The corporate studies group IIPA), 1984.

B. Jalan, Production in tiny, small and large-scale enterprises; A note, *Economic and Political Weekly*, May 20, 1978.

M. Kidron, *Foreign investments in India*, London (Oxford University Press), 1965.

G.K. Lieten (ed.), *The Dutch multinational corporations in India*, New Delhi (Manohar), 1987.

R. Nagaraj, Sub-contracting in Indian manufacturing industries: Analysis, evidence and issues, *Economic and Political Weekly*, august (annual number), 1984.

B. Rajender & G.K. Lieten, The sovereign power of Philips in India, *Social Scientist*, march 1985.

A.K. Rath, Unilever in India, *Social Scientist*, october, 1982.

R. Sau, *India's economic development; Aspects of class relations*, New Delhi (Orient Longman), 1980.

F. van der Velden, Wages of workers in Dutch multinational corporations, *National Labour Institute Bulletin*, no. 3, 1984, pp. 95-104.

F. van der Velden, *Ancillarisation by subsidiaries of Dutch companies in India, Is small beautiful?*, New Delhi/Nijmegen (to be published).

Chapter 5

DEPENDENT INDUSTRIALISATION

Detlev Haude

The focus of this chapter is the *economic development* in *developing countries*. It examines the role international firms are playing in this process on the one hand and that of national industrialisation strategies on the other. We will look into the question of how these processes are reflected in the evolving theories and we will have a cautious look at what the future holds in store.

THEORETICAL BACKGROUNDS

The years following World War II were, amongst other things, characterized by two significant processes: firstly, the *political independenceD of the former colonies now acting on the world market as independent units, and secondly, the emergence of the Newly Industrialising CountriesD (NICs) at a later stage.*

In the 1950s the concept of economic development was chiefly determined by the *Modernization Theory*. It propagated the way of industrialisation adopted by the Western countries, specifically by Europe and the United States, as a model for Third World countries of how to attain a similar level of prosperity. In practice however, this theory proved almost inoperable if not totally inoperable. The majority of the new nations in the Third World were lagging behind in their industrial and agricultural development. Consequently, it did not take long before Modernization Theory was severely criticized. The *Dependency Theory* of various schools of thought suggested that as a consequence of their ties with industrialised Western countries, the development of Third World countries was not feasible. Former colonial power structures would be continued in a new form of control and exploitation, which would prevent these countries from conquering underdevelopment with their own resources. According to Dependency theorists, a major part in this process of continuous underdevelopment is being played by the *international firms*, which are said to have largely taken over the role of the colonial states. Together with the theory of a *Non-CapitalistD or Third Way* based on Marxism and the experiences of the Socialist countries, the Dependency theorists advocated separating the developing countries from the world market. This would allow for a self-generated industrialisation. Participating in the world market and tolerating international firms in their economies would only replicate the process of underdevelopment.

While at universities and in development organizations the various theories and development strategies were still the subjects of heated discussions, industrialisation processes were taking place in some Third World countries challenging current theories and destroying the image of a monomorphic "Third World".

THE NEWLY INDUSTRIALISING COUNTRIES

In particular Singapore, Hong Kong, South Korea and Taiwan, which are all Asian countries, hold good as examples of an NIC. Compared to the "big tiger" Japan they are called the "four small tigers"! In Latin America, Mexico, Brazil, Venezuela and, to a lesser extent, Argentina experienced a surge of industrialisation. There are (still) no NICs on the African continent. Occasionally, in our close environs, Spain, Greece and Turkey are considered parts of this group. Just this enumeration as it is demonstrates the great diversity even within the group of NICs itself. To make the picture even more colourful, the past five year have also distinguished some near-NICs, which may, as is expected, rise to NIC status. In Asia these are Malaysia, Thailand and Indonesia and in Africa the Ivory Coast and Kenya. It is obvious that besides the NICs and the *near-NICs* there is also a large group of Third World countries with little or no industrialisation.

In contrast to these countries, the features of industrialisation of the NICs are the following *common developments* and *structures*. The proportion of the population working in agriculture has dropped considerably and it is smaller than the proportion of the labour force employed in industry and the service sector. Within the GNP, manufacture has displaced agriculture as the relatively most important form of production. Likewise, in foreign trade industrial commodities figure more largely than raw materials from agriculture and mining. Moreover, and this is probably the central fact, the NICs have managed to develop domestic markets within their boundaries which are as important as, or even more important for the selling of industrial commodities than, foreign trade. Besides these analogies between NICs with respect to industrialisation and the position on the world market, similar political structures also exist which have allowed for this development and have promoted it. In all NICs the Government is a major influence on economic activities. At different stages of the industrialisation process governments have deliberately stimulated the growth of home markets (import substitution) and/or the promotion of exports. State enterprises supported, if necessary, the emergence of industry, agricultural reforms were announced and carried out from above and foreign economic relations were subjected to a thorough examination by the official bodies (see chapter 1).

Apart from structural similarities however, not to be neglected are the *differences* which those Third World countries whose economies have experienced a rapid and pervasive growth are displaying. At first it should be pointed out that in each individual country industrialisation took a different course. Thus, with a longer history of independence, the Latin American countries, for instance, had known several periods of industrial growth and decline. From the very beginning Hong Kong and Singapore, small nation states, were more oriented towards the world market than, for example, South Korea and Taiwan. Eventually attention could be drawn to the various industries which were the base and driving force of industrialisation in the NICs. In the Asian countries these were in the early stages mainly the textile and clothing industry and later the steelwork and electrical sector. Initially in Brazil, the extraction of oil and consequent industries played a major role. A last case in point is the oil extraction in the Arab countries, which laid a basis for the petrochemicals industry.

Another difference highlighted in this chapter is the part *internationalfirmsD have played in the industrialisation process of the NICs. In Singapore international firms helped build a service, a petrochemicals and an electrical sector, resulting in a 95-percent control of international firms over this nation state's manufacture. A similar development took place in Hong Kong. In contrast, the industrialisation strategy pursued in South Korea and Taiwan initially implied protection of the domestic market and emerging industry, only later it tolerated firms operating internationally. Thus, in South Korea the share of multinational enterprises in manufacture is about 45 percent, and as far as Taiwan is concerned, it is approximately 43 percent. Brazil adopted the Triple Alliance*, an industrialisation policy under which the Government allots different parts of the industrialisation process to *international firms*, the *indigenous bourgeoisie* and *state-controlled enterprises*. Controlled from above, the collaboration of these partners, each with different knowledge, should provide for stable industrialisation.

Although varying positions occupied by international firms are in evidence in the different stages of industrialisation in individual NICs, the conclusion can be drawn that *eventually* they have an impact on *all* countries. It seems that in the long run the international firm is an inevitable fact within world economy and the industrialisation process of individual countries.

INTERNATIONAL FIRMS AND CONCENTRATION PROCESSES

In classic economic theory the assumption was that the world market was made up of a great many relations between individual *countries* each exploiting its specific advantages in mutual trade, yet today the *international firmsD have to be taken into account (see chapter 1). Relatively separate from the "state" as a political entity, it is evident that they have home countries from which they direct their worldwide activities. It holds true for international firms that their networks made up of producing companies, commercial houses, information channels, research institutions and also financial operations have spread over almost all countries of the world. Not insignificantly, they largely determine the economic dynamics of developed as well as developing countries.*

Two factors are crucial for this leading role: the *geographical spread of their activitiesD and the capital concentration process*. The latter is a continuing process taking place within the developed Capitalist countries. During the economic "boom" after World War II, the main characteristic of the purchase of competing companies and the merge of enterprises was a great variety among the companies concerned. In the so-called *conglomerate* a wide range of industrial activities of the concern were housed under one roof. During the last decade this has been subject to change. International firms have been expanding their core activities more efficiently and they have scrapped those parts of the concern which are not consistent with the company's strategy: a *specialization processD is taking place.*

With respect to the geographical spread, specifically the penetration into Capitalist countries was at issue in the postwar years. In particular United States' investments in Europe and in the European Community were typical of this period. Investments in the former colonies were less significant. This has changed as well. It was pointed out that the prospering NIC economies drew the attention of international firms, however, these firms can also be found in other Third World countries. Apart from interests in raw materials from agriculture and mining (more important in the colonial past than today), growing outlets in the Third World are arousing interest as well. Recent developments have underlined this tendency to internationalize national economies. NIC-based companies intending to expand their activities beyond the size of their home markets and finding their exports hampered by tariff walls erected in, for instance, the European Community, the United States and Japan are introducing their production lines in precisely those countries. Moreover, firms from NICs and near-NICs have started playing the same role in the other Third World countries as their models from the "old" Capitalist countries. Once their domestic resources became exhausted, Philippine forestry enterprises invested in Indonesia. Textile companies from Hong Kong and Taiwan relocated (part of) their production lines in, for instance, Sri Lanka to guarantee their export quotas in this way. National electronics companies from the aforementioned countries are setting up subsidiaries in the United States or are purchasing firms there to gain access to the biggest outlet and to join in with the latest technology.

Ohmae, a Japanese economist, has outlined a future picture of world economy in which enterprises from his native country would control Asia, firms from the European Community, Africa and those of the United States, Latin America. This "redivision" of the world seems somewhat too static. It is not just international firms from the Capitalist countries which are spreading their activities on a global scale, also newcomers from the NICs and the near-NICs are meanwhile taking part in the race for the world market. Of course, expressed in absolute figures and compared to firms from the Capitalist countries, the manufacture of firms from the NICs and the near-NICs is falling behind considerably. Yet, over the past three decades they have realized a spectacular growth and have been active in all fields. It was said that just a few limited "gaps" in the world markets were left for these enterprises, so far facts have proved otherwise. But in the competition for raw materials, labour and outlets they are actually facing their models, which are much larger, and have a longer experience and enormous resources in the form of money, know-how and labour.

NATIONAL STATES AND INTERNATIONAL FIRMS

As mentioned before, the Government's influence in the industrialisation process of Third World countries was crucial. In Europe and the United States the transition from a feodal to a Capitalist economy had been supported mainly by the bourgeoisie. This group gave an impetus to the accumulation process by trade activities, loans at interest, exploitation of colonies and especially so by introducing manufactories. Thus, the bourgeoisie controlled capital and labour factors. It was only later that Government had a regulating function in this process. Economic development was closely linked with the emergence of the civil, democratic state which was to succeed the feodal class society.

Whereas in Europe this process had taken long time, in the former colonies political independence was, as it were, gained in one go. Apparently, this situation helped create opportunities of taking advantage of all past experiences in the development process. It explains why "free entrepreneurship" from the West, planning experience from the Soviet Union and the specific mode of development of secluded Japan can be recognized in their various forms in Third World countries. It appears that planning has been the main difference from Western industrialisation. Government's influence in the development programme was much stronger. It directed the accumulation process by introducing state enterprises and interfering in the private sector and it did not confine itself to a regulating role. In the Socialist developing countries, of course, this was the dominant line, whereas in other countries the planning function of Government was considered a necessary support of the private sector. Considering that, after all, the ideology of these development-oriented nations, such as the NICs, was free entrepreneurship, it is logical that the government influence in economic development had been forced back at a later stage.

It is interesting to note that the term *deregulation*, i.e. government withdrawal from direct economic interests, has also become common currency in the developed countries. The two phenomena differ in their historical backgrounds and in the effects on the economies and the societies concerned. Yet they are both pointing to one and the same tendency in both types of countries: an increasing privatization of economic activities.

During a period of globally extending networks of international firms and government withdrawal from economic functions it seems that, more than ever, the future is going to be determined by firms operating worldwide. All the same, these companies still need a home base to control their networks and to coordinate their production and selling strategies. As long as there are nations competing with one another, the contrast between nations on the one hand and international company networks on the other will remain.

Two examples illustrate that the focus which used to be on the performance of a national economy has been shifted to the international firm: *Made in Germany* used to stand for the quality of the product, at the same time it reflected some kind of nationalism. Even now this sign can still be found on a Volkswagen. But has this car in fact been made there? Volkswagen components (and components of other famous brands) may come from different countries and also be assembled there. What remains is the concept of Volkswagen guaranteeing a commodity manufactured and sold worldwide, but its label, *Made in Germany*, has lost its original meaning. The same thing applies to, for instance, commodities in the electronics sector and foodstuffs. The significance of international firms for a national economy used to be denoted by the sentence: "*What is good for General Motors is good for the United States*". Now that components for their automobiles are supplied to Detroit by Mexican factories, this sentence has lost its meaning in political-geographical respect.

The second example concerns measures other than economic by which managements expect the company to hold on tight to their employees, such as attempts to create a sort of "company culture" encouraging employees to company loyalty and better performance. No longer does it seem to matter where in the world one is working for IBM. What is important is that one feels part of the company's global network.

THE INTERNATIONAL FIRM: AN INEVITABLE FACTOR

The internationalization of manufacture and the expansion of the world market fuelled by international firms does not imply that the significance of the Government has been reduced: her role is changing.

Just as the close attachment of people with their companies in *Japan* has served in part as a model, the relation existing between large international firms in this country _ *the shogo soshas*_ could function as a guideline for other countries. In Japan the Government does not have any direct interest in the companies, but it stimulates the expansion of firms by political and financial measures. Hence, the Government's position is very strong not in fact by exercising a direct but an indirect influence on the economy. An identical construction can be recognized in, for instance, *South Korean* economy in which the Government helped set up large conglomerates _ the *chaebols* _ in the private sector. Similar strategies have been adopted by other NIC countries and near-NICs, but often less successfully. In *Indonesia*, where since 1965 the Suharto regime have pursued a nationalist and meanwhile Western-oriented industrialisation strategy, the "*joint venture*" is figuring largely. It implies that the foreign firm and her Indonesian partner are supplying capital and know-how to a shared company, supported by financial and infrastructural government measures. This form of investment by international firms in Third World countries is more and more displacing the subsidiary entirely controlled by a foreign company. The *joint ventureD is profitable to both partners. Firstly, risk is spread and secondly, it gives in to nationalist sentiments voicing attacks on new forms of dependency for ex-colonies.*

The last mentioned consideration is likely to play a role at the opening of *Socialist economies[1] to international firms. Even in the past countries such as Yugoslavia* and *Hungary* entered into cooperations with firms from the West. Yet, the most spectacular example was the least expected: international firms from the Capitalist core countries and other developed countries were granted admission to the *People's Republic of China.* At present *joint venturesD are being introduced in almost all sectors of Chinese economy. This process of Chinese economic participation in the world market coincides with a far-reaching liberalization. With some reservation the Soviet Union* sees a similar process being started in which the *joint venture* is called *common enterprise.* Other countries such as *Vietnam, AngolaD and Mozambique* have enacted laws on investment which enable foreign companies to invest in these Socialist countries. In fact, rather than discouraging such investments, these countries are waiting for them.

A last development showing the international interrelationship of national economies through firms operating worldwide is the investments from *JapanD and the NICs in the United States and the European Community. What applied to investments from the Western countries throughout the 1950s and 1960s applies equally to these investments: trade barriers and (potential) out-*

lets on which a lengthy export period has done its "preliminary work" make direct investment advisable if not necessary.

These initiatives to an advancing industrialisation of world economy in which the leading part is not restricted to firms from the Capitalist countries alone strongly underline the inevitable role of the international firm. Hence, there will be no future for nationalist attacks either in the Third World on domination by Western companies or in the West on "alien" companies from the NICs which are flooding the markets with their inexpensive goods.

The discrepancy which may arise between national economies and international company networks is highlighted by the painstaking way in which, initiated by the Government, *supranational markets* are being realized, whereas the nations concerned have been impregnated by company networks even for long time. Regional markets such as those suggested by the Andes agreement in South America, the West African market or the ASEAN (a cooperation of South-east Asian countries), have either had no impact or have hardly been able to reach their key targets of the integration of national economies. The European Community, too, are having difficulties in their pursuit of a total dismantling of the barriers between their member states. A few years ago some Managing Directors of international European firms thought this to be sufficient reason to join forces and form a pressure group to accelerate integration.

THE WORLD AS A SOURCE AND A MARKET

Even more than one decade ago Adam and Hymer, both economists, characterized the strategy as pursued in international firms with the term "*worldwide sourcing*". Production factors such as raw materials, (skilled) labour, transport and outlets are integrated into a concern structure dependent on their interrelations on a global scale. Political systems and economic legislations are equally important. Central characteristics of the development of the world market since World War II have been the transfer of production lines from the home country of a company to another place and the incorporation of foreign companies into the concern structure. Owing to the surge of industrialisation sketched above and some technological innovations this development became possible (see chapter 1).

As a result of faster and standardized possibilities of transport the world seemed to shrink. Close geographical connections between locations of production and outlets were less necessary. This process was reinforced by a far-reaching fragmentation of production processes allowing for a wider spread. These phenomena are related to the emergence of information technology enabling spread activities to be integrated. Competition between enterprises resulted in the distribution of the latest technology on a global scale.

Related to these economic-technological transition processes in Capitalist countries as well as NICs and near-NICs, a spending pattern developed which transcended regional and/or national markets with respect to particular commodities: a kind of *world cultureD with a world supermarket* was created. This trend can especially be observed in the consumer goods sector.

THE LABOUR FACTOR

The above attempt at an outline of the transition processes put an emphasis on company as well as world level. This implicitly shows some of the effects for the people, particularly for those employed within the networks of international firms. The following sections try to give some further details on the issue.

Developments in the relocated industries in particular, that is, in textiles and electronics in Europe and in automobile industry in the United States, gave rise to the question: will jobs be lost in the Capitalist countries if production lines are transferred to Third World countries? Are the effects of competition from

NIC and near-NIC-based industries on employment in the West not just as negative? It is impossible to answer these two questions *unequivocally*. They contain just one single factor whereas in real terms there are several factors involved in the transfer of production lines and employment loss. Also labour unions working on these issues, for example, in the Netherlands, West Germany, the United States and Australia, have not been able to find the final answer. A preliminary hypothesis, formulated with all reservation, might be this: jobs losses in particular industries in the West concern sectors and branches which, with respect to the Capitalist development stage there, are outdated. They will either largely disappear or they need to be changed by new technologies. For some time industrialising Third World countries had specific advantages, (such as low wages and grants), which enabled them to attract these industries, however, they will have to switch over to new technologies and commodities almost as soon as the Western countries. The reason for putting it this way is the phenomenon of the *re-run-away-industries*, that is, the industries which "come back home again". Owing to automation and robotization of manufacture, this reverse move of, for example, electronics and textile companies is made possible. This is why low wages are going to be a factor of minor importance in the company strategy. This development is also apparent in the NICs. In Singapore and Hong Kong, which are greatly dependent of the international market, and in South Korea and Taiwan, which have to meet with international competition, national and international firms are already changing over to automation of their previously labour-intensive industries.

To make things clear, some features of Japanese economy should be pointed out once more. The most advanced production lines are to be found at the top; they employ highly qualified people working on appointments in technologically highly advanced labour environments. These enterprises are floating, as it were, on a sea of small supplying companies, often family businesses. The pressure to rationalize and reduce costs even more is forcing automation upon precisely these buyer-dependent companies as a result of which redundancies are likely to occur in an already unstable employment situation.

It would be premature to say that the future of all industrialised societies is going to be determined by the phenomenon of a relatively small group of "permanent" employees facing a massive group of "temporary" workers. It is equally conceivable that precisely the impetus given to smaller industrial units will result in more jobs, provided that unilateral dependency of important buyers can be avoided. What is characteristic of the transition processes outlined above is the great variety of types of work on the shop-floor occurring in this stage of Capitalist development. Part-time work, home-working and other forms of subcontracting are on the increase (see chapter 1).

In the internationalization process of Capitalist manufacture the labour factor remains quite immobile. The fragmentation and the mobility of production processes make it possible to by-pass the relative immobility of the employee by integrating various types of labour into different parts of one company network. This way allows for adjustments to shifts in the production process. Furthermore, new technologies can be introduced at that place in the organization of manufacture where they fit in best. At the same time it is also possible to go along with the different economic and political interest of the employees concerned. Permanent employment, temporary jobs, seasonal labour and home-working can often be found in one concern.

The increasing exchange of higher personnel who get familiar with situations in various countries is in sharp contrast with the circumstances on the shop-floor where one can scarcely maintain relationships with people abroad. Regarding the various interests and the social and cultural backgrounds of the employees, it will be hard to realize the idea of firm-oriented labour unions, though they remain advisable because of the internationalization of the enterprises themselves.

DEPENDENT OR RELATED INDUSTRIALISATION

When, in the 1950s, the concept of the Third World was introduced in France denoting the newly-politically independent colonies, it seemed easy to analyse and describe the situation. There was a *First*, industrialised world, a *Second*, Socialist world, and a *Third*, economically dependent one. The two theories mentioned at the beginning of this chapter, the Modernization and the Dependency Theory, were diametrically opposed. The choice for one of the two was easy, it was determined by political inclination.

Three decades later such a choice is no longer conceivable. Some Third World countries are largely industrialised (*the NICs*) or are in one of the final stages of the industrialisation process (the *near-NICs*). Other countries are also differing to such an extent that their economic structures can no longer be placed under one common heading. A great many countries are still dependent on the export of raw materials and the majority of the people in the countryside or in the city are living in wretched conditions. No longer, to be sure, can the term "Third World" be used to denote a conglomerate of countries showing more differences than similarities in their socio-economic structures and political ideologies.

To make a *political* choice has become equally difficult. Planning alone is insufficient as the experiences of Socialist-orientated countries have proved. Conversely, the strategy of NICs is challenging those theorists who pointed to the examples of the West and the "free market". Besides, transition processes taking place in highly developed Capitalist countries as well as NICs are providing counterevidence to the assumption that there is just one single pattern through which Capitalist development can be achieved. This appears from, amongst other things, several types of work emerging or re-emerging worldwide at the present stage of economic change. Finally, the theorists pleading for a separation from the world market have proved to be biased just as those seeing advantages only in the integration of a national economies into the world market.

In the *evolving theories* this situation is reflected, for instance, in the works of Wallerstein, an American historian. He conceives the rise and decline of economic powers in the form of national states in het course of history, however, at the same time he sticks to a classification of countries into *core* (highly developed Capitalist countries), *semi-peripheralD (e.g. the NICs) and peripheral* countries (with no industrial development of any consequence). In relation to stringent Modernization and Dependency Theories this is definitely a step forward. The question remains whether this new model is still too narrow. The rise of industrialising countries and the relative decline of great powers also allows for the notion that a Capitalist world (market) may emerge in which after an *"old" and a new international division of labour an interrelated division of labour* may occur. Within this framework large differences which still exist between individual countries would disappear and a more balanced structure between countries would emerge. Yet, such a notion still does not take account of international firms to a satisfactory degree. Besides interests of national units and regional subunits, their influence is essential to economic change.

An attempt was made to point to the question of how these changes came about on the concrete level of city and region in this book for Nijmegen and its surrounding areas. At an abstract level Nijmegen and environs could be compared with some regions in developing countries concerning its late industrialisation, little differentiation in its economy and the increasing influence of international firms on its economic structure. One could do this as well with respect to the function of the regional authorities in attracting companies from outside. Obviously, an equal status, i.e. *Nijmegen = Third World*, is not suggested. It is true that this type of comparison of problems arising in a region in an industrialised country with the developmental problems of a Third World country may show that, by taking positions in opposition to international firms, regions are competing with each other in their pursuit of economic change and growth. Concurrently, this comparison raises a few questions concerning labour union strategies. How can unions be equipped for this rapidly changing situation? And how can they coordinate their national strategies at an international level? This remains a challenge for the unions as well as for the scholar who does not think that analysis alone is beneficial or conclusive.

Selected bibliography

P. Dicken, *Global shift; Industrial change in a turbulent world*, London (Harper & Row), 1986.

P. Evans, *Latin America in the World Economy*, Aldershot (Gower Press), 1983.

F. Fröbel, J. Heinrichs, O. Kreye, *The New International Division of Labour: Structural Unemployment in the industrial countries and industrialisation in developing countries*, Cambridge (CUP), 1980 (or. in german 1977).

idem, *Umbruch in der Weltwirtschaft*, Reinbek bei Hamburg (Rowohlt), 1986.

C. Hamilton, Capitalist industrialisation in East Asia's Four Little Tigers, *Journal of Contemporary Asia*, vol. 13, no. 1, 1983, p. 35-73.

N. Harris, *The end of the Third World. Newly industrialising countries and the decline of an ideology*, Harmondsworth (Penguin), 1987.

D. Haude, Transnationale Unternehmen, Industrialisierung in der Peripherie und kapitalistische Entwicklung, *Peripherie. Zeitschrift für Politik und Ökonomie in der Dritten Welt*, no. 21, summer 1985, p. 6-24.

idem, Von Agrikultur zur Agroindustrie, *Peripherie. Zeitschrift für Politik und Ökonomie in der Dritten Welt*, no. 28, spring 1987, p. 51-86.

Th. Hurtienne, Fordismus, Entwicklungstheorie und Dritte Welt, *Peripherie. Zeitschrift für Politik und Ökonomie in der Dritten Welt*, no. 22/23, fall/winter 1985/86, p. 60-110.

G. Junne ed., New technologies and Third World development, *Vierteljahres-berichte des Forschungsinstituts der Friedrich-Ebert Stiftung*, no. 103, march 1986.

A. Lipietz, Imperialism or the beast of the Apocalypse, *Capital & Class*, no. 22, spring 1984, p. 81-109.

J. Saravanamuttu, Imperialism, dependent development and ASEAN regionalism, *Journal of Contemporary Asia*, vol. 16, no. 2, 1986, p. 204-222.

I. Wallerstein, *The capitalist world economy*, Cambridge (CUP), 1979.

K. Ohmae, *Triad Power. The coming shape of global competition*, The Free Press (Glencoe), 1985.

Appendix I

LIST OF FIRMS IN THE NIJMEGEN REGION RELATED TO A MULTINATIONAL CORPORATION

The following list is meant to give an indication of which major multinationals are represented in the Nijmegen region to readers abroad.

The first line gives the name of the industrial firm in the Nijmegen region, the second one its mother company or majority owner. The situation is that of 1985.

Koninklijke Brinkers Margarinefabrieken B.V., Wijchen	Kon. Brinkers Margarinefabrieken B.V., Zoetermeer (NL)
Celtona B.V., Katwijk (Cuijk)	Bührmann Tetterode N.V., Amsterdam (NL)
Chicopee B.V., Cuijk	Johnson & Johnson, New Brunswick (USA)
Colt International B.V., Cuijk	Colt International Ltd., Havant, Hants., (UK)
C.S.M. Honig B.V., Nijmegen	Centrale Suiker Maatschappij N.V., Amsterdam (NL)

Nederlandse Philips Bedrijven B.V., Nijmegen	N.V. Philips Gloeilampenfabrieken, Eindhoven (NL)
Printronix B.V., Wijchen	Printronix Inc., Irvine, California (USA)
Renco International B.V., Wijchen	United Brands Company, Boston, Mass., (USA)
Scaldia Papier B.V., Nijmegen	Financière Intermills SA., (Belgium)
Sealed Air B.V., Nijmegen	Sealed Air Corporationm Danbury, C.T., (USA)
Smit Transformatoren B.V., Nijmegen	Holec N.V., Utrecht (NL), 50% employees, 50%
Smitweld B.V., Nijmegen	Norgas AS, (Norway)
Van Swaay-Garantor B.V., Nijmegen	Internatio Müller N.V., Rotterdam (NL)
Synbra Unie B.V., Wijchen	Shell, 50% (NL-UK)
Thompack B.V., Weurt	Borden Inc. International, New York (USA)
Verzinkerij Mook B.V., Mook	TBI Holdings, Rotterdam (NL)

Acknowledgements

We are grateful to all the people who have helped with the writing of this book. In the first place we would like to thank those students who did research finally leading to the publication of the Dutch book mentioned before and whose contributions are referred to in the third chapter of this edition: Peter van den Akker (Philips), Benny Beernink and Michel Michon (Nutricia).

We also wish to thank those students who participated in the course and the research but whose papers were not published in the end. We are grateful to Elly Galama for her patience in translating the Dutch (and often Double Dutch) texts into English and to Wilbert Kruijsen for his efforts to provide the lay-out of this publication.